Beyond Neoliberalism and Neo-illiberalism

Economic Policies and Performance
for Sustainable Democracy

THE NEW | Volume 1

THE NEW publishes collaborative research in the humanities and social sciences. Its publications offer future-oriented responses to the nested crises of the present along the dimensions of what it means to be human, how to improve democratic self-governance, and how to achieve socio-economic transformation. Our goal is to make humanistic research relevant and accessible to wider audiences.

Beyond Neoliberalism and Neo-illiberalism

Economic Policies and Performance
for Sustainable Democracy

Edited by:
Markus Gabriel, Anna Katsman,
Thomas Liess, and William Milberg

THE NEW INSTITUTE   [transcript]

Bibliographic information published by the Deutsche Nationalbibliothek

The Deutsche Nationalbibliothek lists this publication in the Deutsche Nationalbibliografie; detailed bibliographic data are available in the Internet at https://dnb.dnb.de

This work is licensed under the Creative Commons Attribution-ShareAlike 4.0 (BY-SA) which means that the text may be remixed, built upon and be distributed, provided credit is given to the author and that copies or adaptations of the work are released under the same or similar license. For details go to https://creativecommons.org/licenses/by-sa/4.0/

Creative Commons license terms for re-use do not apply to any content (such as graphs, figures, photos, excerpts, etc.) not original to the Open Access publication and further permission may be required from the rights holder. The obligation to research and clear permission lies solely with the party re-using the material.

First published in 2024 by transcript Verlag, Bielefeld
© Markus Gabriel, Anna Katsman, Thomas Liess, William Milberg (eds.) and the authors

Design & Typesetting: Maciej Kodzis, CDLX GmbH and THE NEW INSTITUTE

Copy-editing: Diana Perry Schnelle

Printed by: Friedrich Pustet GmbH & Co. KG, Regensburg

Print-ISBN 978-3-8376-7487-3
PDF-ISBN 978-3-8394-7487-7
EPUB-ISBN 978-3-7328-7487-3

https://doi.org/10.14361/9783839474877

ISSN of series: 2510-9286
eISSN of series: 2510-9294

Printed on permanent acid-free text paper.

	Editorial	Markus Gabriel and Anna Katsman, THE NEW INSTITUTE	9
	Introductions	William Milberg, The New School	13
		Laura Carvalho, Open Society Foundations	19
		Brian Kettenring, Hewlett Foundation	23
I	The Connection Between Economy and Democracy	**After Neoliberalism,** Dani Rodrik	27
		Illiberal Political Economics after Neoliberalism, Jessica Pisano	35
		Pursuing a Human Rights Economy, Darrick Hamilton	41
		Markets and Democracy, Joseph Stiglitz	47
II	Drivers of Neo-illiberalism	**Why and How Precarious Workers Support Neo-illiberalism,** Rosana Pinheiro-Machado	59
		Austerity: Why, What, and How – Lessons from the UK's Failed Experiment, Thiemo Fetzer	79
		The Enduring Social and Economic Consequences of the China Trade Shock, David Autor	89

III	Policy and Performance in the Illiberal Turn: Money and Growth	**Populist Leadership and Economic Decline**, Moritz Schularick, Christoph Trebesch, and Manuel Funke	113
		The Politics and Limits of Monetary Policy Under Growing Authoritarianism: The Case of Turkey, Ayca Zayim	125
		Illiberalism on Europe's Periphery: A Critical Macrofinance Tale, Daniela Gabor	149
IV	Policy and Performance in the Illiberal Turn: Labor Market and Social Protection	**The Labor and Social Policies of Neo-authoritarian Populist Governments: A Comparative Analysis of Hungary, Poland, and Türkiye**, Janine Berg and Ludovica Tursini	177
		Corporate Majoritarianism in India, Sheba Tejani	201
	Conclusion	**Towards a Democratic Economics**, William Milberg, The New School	223
	List of Contributors		227

Editorial

THE NEW publishes collaborative research in the humanities and social sciences. Its publications offer future-oriented responses to the nested crises of the present along the dimensions of what it means to be human, how to improve democratic self-governance, and how to achieve socio-economic transformation.

This publication arose out of a workshop on *Rethinking Capitalism: Creating Value for Social Well-Being*, which took place at THE NEW INSTITUTE in Hamburg from September 5–7, 2023. Within the framework of the fundamental themes that the Institute addresses – the human condition in the 21st century, the future of democracy, and socio-economic transformation – we discussed what future of democracy is worth wanting, what future is available, and how can we account for the rapid rise of authoritarian regimes. The discussion turned again and again to how the neoliberal economic policies of the past decades have been essential drivers of the crisis of democracy and how this crisis has led to the rise of a novel socio-economic constellation, which the authors contributing to this publication discuss as "neo-illiberalism". Some of the authors were present at our workshop. Given the overlap between the concerns of THE NEW INSTITUTE and the essays assembled by Will Milberg and Thomas Liess here, we are delighted to publish recent work being done on the economic, political, and cultural consequences of neoliberalism and the rise of neo-illiberalism.

The papers in this publication explore concrete cases from around the world in order to identify the hallmarks of the neo-illiberal constellation of democracy and capitalist market societies. As Milberg sums it up, the papers collectively "point to the need for a more sustained effort to counter both the economic insecurity and volatility of neoliberalism and the labor suppression, ethno-nationalism and clientelism of the neo-illiberal economies. Such an effort will require creative and interdisciplinary work on both theory and policy" (this volume, p. 223). As we saw during our *Rethinking Capitalism* workshop, this effort to effectively counter neo-illiberalism will depend on opening up a space for a novel reconfiguration of the liberal self-conception of the human.

At THE NEW INSTITUTE, we believe the humanities and social sciences provide realistic yet value-laden conceptions of the human that avoid fallacies, simplifications, and other ideological traps. Only on this basis will it be possible to shape the future of capitalism by democratic means without falling prey to the reductionist conception of the human being and its economic rationality promoted under neoliberalism. The discipline of economics must be recoupled with the humanities to support value judgments of a broader and ultimately ethical kind. The evidence clearly suggests that ethno-nationalist, neo-illiberal economic policies undermine social well-being at least as much as the unleashing of a one-sided, neoliberal, dualistic opposition of market and state, human being and nature, social self-consciousness and our animality. Thus, while neoliberalism has failed by not embedding markets within a cultural and institutional context geared towards social well-being, neo-illiberalism will certainly do no better. At most, neo-illiberalism achieves short-term investment in stereotypes around which fictions of national, ethnic, religious, and other identities cluster so that they can be politically exploited in the pursuit of consolidating more political power in the hands of actors who fear the sovereignty of the people.

We thank Will Milberg and Thomas Liess for offering us this exciting collection of essays, for which they serve as editors. We also thank the Open Society Foundations and the Hewlett Foundation for their support of the projects that led to this publication.

The papers assembled here present research by leading economists, sociologists, and political scientists who interrogate the intersections between the future of democracy and capitalism that are driving the troubling socio-economic transformations we are witnessing. These papers serve as models for international and transdisciplinary cooperation based on informed research that provides normative orientation in complex times – without which we will not be able to shape the future or contribute to positive social change. Complex situations require complex solutions. We hope that these essays will inspire our readers by providing them with a novel take on our present moment, which points beyond neoliberalism and neo-illiberalism alike.

MARKUS
GABRIEL
THE NEW INSTITUTE

ANNA
KATSMAN
THE NEW INSTITUTE

Introductions

This publication of THE NEW – *Beyond Neoliberalism and Neo-illiberalism: Economic Policies and Performance for Sustaining Democracy*, presents papers from a convening held on March 27th and 28th, 2023 at The New School for Social Research. It features an informative and wide-ranging discussion of a number of basic questions on the relation between democracy and economy. The political backlash against neoliberalism has mainly been a retreat from democracy. Its main features are the decline in independence of the judiciary and the monetary authorities, suppression, or control of the media, and, of course, direct manipulation of election rules for purposes of authoritarian control.

The causes of this authoritarian shift are many, of which the economic dynamics and the impact of deregulation and liberalized markets – neoliberalism – are just one. Although there are many studies of the causes of democratic "backsliding" and "neo-illiberalism", there has been inadequate attention to the economic consequences of the neo-illiberal turn. With its grants to The New School for Social Research, the Open Society Foundations and the Hewlett Foundation have supported the advancement of thinking on the economics of neo-illiberalism that has been seen across a variety of countries. The project has been enormously generative in raising questions about the role of neoliberal economic policies in relation to other cultural and political factors in promoting the recent authoritarian turn, as well as about the commonalities in the economic policies and economic performance of the illiberal regimes.

The convening featured research on Turkey, India, Hungary, Poland, the Philippines, Bolsonaro's Brazil, Trump's America, and Brexit in the UK. Three themes stood out in our deliberations: (1) the role of neoliberal economic policies in relation to other cultural and political factors in promoting the recent authoritarian turn in many democracies; (2) the challenges, inequities, and disappointments of the economic policies and economic performance of the neo-illiberal regimes; and (3) the need to develop positive alternatives to the unsatisfactory performance of both neoliberal economic policy and the neo-illiberal policy frameworks we observed. The first two questions were addressed on the first day of the conference and the third was the focus of an intensive discussion the second day. I return to (3) in the conclusion of this report.

To open the issue, Dani Rodrik argues that "hyperglobalization" was one of the causes of the anti-democratic backlash. He proposes that the world trading system return to something more like the General Agreement on Tariffs and Trade (GATT), focusing narrowly on tariffs and creating policy space for countries to control other features affected by globalization, including capital flows, competition policy, and taxes. Joseph Stiglitz goes further, arguing that free markets had created outcomes – unsustainable debt, financial crises, wage stagnation, precarious employment, and income inequality – that directly induced an anti-democratic turn. He makes the case for strengthening "collective action" to underpin a more democratic approach to growth and development. Darrick Hamilton makes the case for economics to be included as a human right, thus connecting the economic and the political dimensions explicitly. Hamilton calls for "inclusive economic rights…where economic rights become the cornerstone investment in our future and a necessary and inseparable component of human rights." Power asymmetries, associated with race or ethnicity or nationality must be addressed, he argues, if these human rights are to be honored. Jessica Pisano connects economic clientelism to the anti-democratic tendencies observed especially in Eastern Europe. Illiberalism, she claims, often has less ideological content than many imagine, noting that "while illiberalism *produces* something that looks like ethnonationalism, it often *starts* from an economic compact, a transactional politics." She argues that there is a distinct political economy of illiberalism that will have to be addressed if political change is to be accomplished, and this political economy results from the unique relation between central political power and local clientelist dynamics.

Subsequent papers go into specific national examples. Anthropologist Rosana Pinheiro-Machado explores the case of free-market beliefs on the part of low-income platform workers (e.g., Uber drivers) in Brazil, who oppose government anti-poverty measures. Such workers support the free-market, pro-entrepreneur platform of President Bolsonaro because they resent that they often cannot access government support for the poor. They self-identify as entrepreneurs and social media tends to bolster both this sense of entrepreneurial identity, and the unfairness of the welfare system for these "entrepreneurs." David Autor provides detailed evidence that Chinese import penetration into the US resulted in deep, regionally specific impacts to unemployment and manufacturing, associated with increased electoral support for President Trump. Thiemo Fetzer shows that fiscal austerity was associated with the vote on Brexit, but that the role of austerity is relevant to understanding other crises as well, including the Covid-19 pandemic and recent difficulties around energy supply associated with the Russian invasion of Ukraine. Fetzer describes austerity as "a signature zero-sum policy" and identifies the solution in part as one of engaging local communities in research on the natural and social challenges.

The last two papers look at the policies and performance of the new illiberal democracies. Moritz Schularick, Christoph Trebesch and Manuel Funke present a broad econometric study of "populism" since 1900, which shows consistent underperformance in economic growth by (left-wing and right-wing) populist governments compared to how they would have performed in the absence of a populist turn. This is a sobering introduction to papers on macro and monetary policy and on labor market and social protection policy. The challenges of a politically dependent central bank function are discussed in the cases of Turkey and Hungary. Ayca Zayim shows how Turkey's efforts to keep interest rates low as they increased internationally led to debilitating currency depreciation and drastic declines in real income. Daniela Gabor details a similar experience in Hungary and thus the challenge of bucking international financial pressures for clientelist, local capitalist, gains. The lessons are also useful for other countries in the future. Part of the Trump platform for a second term is to limit the independence of the Federal Reserve, according to recent reports.

On the labor market side, Sheba Tejani argues that Modi's support for anti-Muslim movements has been part of a broader "corporate majoritarianism" featuring the elimination of some basic labor rights and economic empowerment of a few political cronies. Janine Berg and Ludovica Tursini find that while labor rights were under attack in Hungary, Poland, and the Philippines, real wage growth in these countries was surprisingly strong.

A goal of this project has been to push the discussion beyond the critique of neoliberalism to also assess the economics of anti-democratic tendencies. The first question was to consider just what the economic policy levers of the new anti-democratic regimes are. Are these economic policies similar across countries to the point where we can identify a coherent "neo-illiberal" economics (the way many have done for neoliberalism)? Are the policies significantly different from those of the neoliberal era? The papers in this special issue indicate that it certainly seems so, with nationalism and xenophobia driving illiberal restrictions on international trade and immigration. The papers have added important detail by focusing on monetary policy, labor market policy, and social protectionism.

The second goal was to assess the effectiveness of the economic policies in these anti-democratic countries. Have the policies been able to generate just and equitable economic outcomes, while sustaining the democratic principles that many of us hold? The evidence presented in the research that went into these papers gives a negative answer to this question. Growth rates are lower than they would otherwise be, clientelism leads to preferential treatment of a political base to the great detriment of minority ethnic groups and immigrants, and the challenges of anti-democratic control can wreak havoc on the macroeconomy.

The overall findings of this important research lead to a next set of questions: If neoliberalism has largely failed and the reaction against it has not been an enormous economic success, then what next? What is an economic model for the future, or even a set of economic policies, we can contemplate for the future of capitalism? These daunting questions will be the subject of the next phase of the project, currently ongoing.

The idea for this project came out of conversations with the Open Society Foundations (OSF) and Hewlett Foundation. It is well known that OSF has been supporting causes that advance democracy for decades, and the Hewlett Foundation has now become a leader in the search for a new economic paradigm, that is, new economic theories that might underpin a democratic and just economic policy regime. I want to thank these foundations for their support for this project. Laura Carvalho (from OSF) and Brian Kettenring (from Hewlett Foundation) each said a word of welcome at the convening and they have kindly agreed to include their introductory comments here. Laura and Brian provided support in terms of funding, but they have been full intellectual partners in this project as well.

WILLIAM
MILBERG
The New School

I think Will Milberg has framed well what the moment requires of us, and the importance of the topic that we will be discussing in this convening. The idea here is, of course, to revisit some of the evidence, and there is a lot of evidence, on the role different economic policies had on the rise of authoritarianism.

In the Global North, there is vast evidence of the importance of globalization and trade, in particular, for what we are seeing in terms of backlash, both from the ethno-nationalist perspective and the far-right and authoritarian platforms in Europe and in the US. But when you look at the Global South, the situation is not necessarily the same. Of course, globalization plays a role there as well and de-industrialization is happening in many parts of the Global South. But we can see a bit of nuance when we think about the role globalization played in countries like Brazil, which benefited from Chinese growth and commodity prices in the 2000s. Nonetheless, we still saw democratic backlash.

This starts to raise some questions around what exactly are the economic policies that haven't delivered and have created fertile ground for these authoritarians in different parts of the world. Maybe there are different roles that have been played by different policies.

By bringing researchers from different parts of the world to this conference, this is one of the first questions that we will try to answer. Of course, there is also evidence of the role of fiscal austerity and labor deregulation. In those cases, we may be able to see more common ground in different countries.

The second aspect that I would like to call attention to is the issue of neo-illiberalism, especially in economic policy. It is true that in this recent wave of authoritarian regimes, we have not had a comprehensive assessment of the economic policies such regimes have been using. Going back to Brazil, Bolsonaro's regime was a combination of authoritarianism and moral conservatism with market fundamentalism. So many would argue that economically it was a very neo-illiberal government. Yet the policies implemented by Bolsonaro's government were actually even more radical neoliberal policies than what the country had seen in the past 20 years.

Brazil's combination of authoritarian politics and neoliberal economics is not necessarily what we have seen in other contexts where there has been a combination of illiberalism and an anti-systemic type of economic policies. And so, the question again emerges: as we try to move to another economic paradigm that can simultaneously deliver benefits to citizens and create the conditions for democracies to thrive, how do we assess the capacity of these governments to deliver?

As The Open Society Foundations' Global Director of Equity, I have been part of this conversation since the beginning, and we are proud to co-host and fund this event together with the Hewlett Foundation. I studied at The New School and graduated with a PhD in economics in 2012, so it is a very special occasion for me and it is great to have so many OSF colleagues and some of my former New School professors in the room.

LAURA
CARVALHO
Open Society Foundations

As the Director of the Economy and Society Initiative at the William and Flora Hewlett Foundation, I lead a five-year $100 million grantmaking effort that aims to foster a "new common sense" about how the economy works, the aims it should serve, and how it should be structured to meet the biggest challenges our society faces. In other words, this initiative seeks to foster a new economic paradigm in terms of what comes after neoliberalism. Initially, this work was conceptualized as part of our democracy work at the foundation, as part of an analysis of how to respond to Trumpism. It came out of a thought process that was domestically oriented, seeking to understand what was happening in the United States.

I think of neoliberalism as a set of ideas and practices buttressed by power. Although such ideas seem to be increasingly in retreat, they remain persistent and embedded, and forces underneath them allow them to stay alive.

In recent years, increasingly, the threat for those of us working in political economy is ethnonationalism. For us, then, this conference marks a bit of a turn to take up the question of ethnonationalism and political economy. In doing so, we have to be as laser focused as ever, as one cannot defeat something with nothing. Hence the need to craft democratic alternatives. To do so, however, we need a more rigorous analysis of what is happening in the relationship between political economy and authoritarianism.

For Hewlett, this convening marks the strategic opening of a conversation. Like you, we have our own questions, which I bring to this conversation. These include:
1. the relationship between inequality, extremism, and alienation;
2. taking up the fallacy that neoliberal opening would lead to democratization;
3. the class inversion within the parties in the United States and parts of the West that is not happening everywhere around the world. What does this mean for political institutions and processes?;

4. Gary Gerstle's 2022 book *The Rise and Fall of the Neoliberal Order: America and the World in the Free Market Era* really underscores the relationship between geopolitics and domestic political economy. He argued, for example, that the Soviet dynamic in the US, the threat of communism, reinforced an inclusive compact between workers and capital in the United States. Given the return of geopolitics, how does that play out?

I would like to thank Laura Carvalho, Mark Malloch Brown, and the team at The Open Society Foundations for their partnership in this project, as well as William Milberg and his team at The New School. We are really eager to be on this journey with you.

BRIAN
KETTENRING
Hewlett Foundation

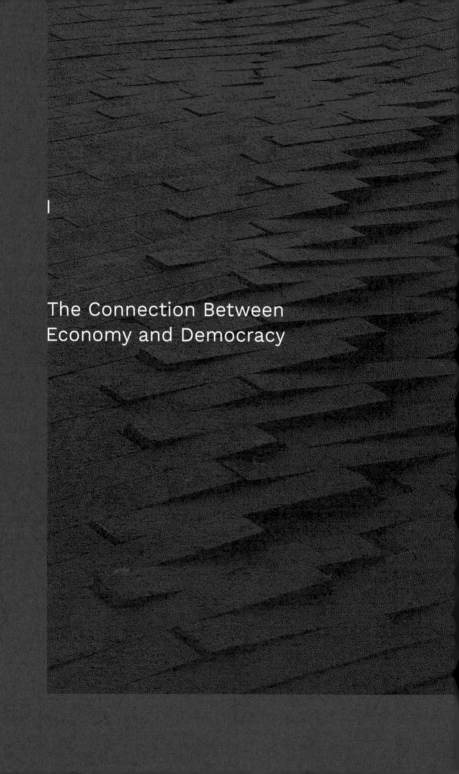

I

The Connection Between
Economy and Democracy

After Neoliberalism[1]

DANI RODRIK
Kennedy School,
Harvard University

This section focuses on what policies would be desirable in a potential economic regime following neoliberalism, and alternative to neo-illiberalism, and it aims to present some of the key features of this new order. Two scenarios are possible, an optimistic one and another more pessimistic. This section will mainly focus on the positive scenario, while raising some concerns about how the system could shift toward a negative one.

There is not a very tight connection between neoliberalism and the political regime type, at least in the short run, rather there might be one over longer or historical stretches. However, one relationship I want to draw attention to concerns the nature of the transformation that labor markets have been going through recently. Indeed, what is happening nowadays in low- and middle-income countries, ranging widely from Eastern Europe to other countries, is very different from the historical processes that created advanced social democracies in today's developed world, and it also results in very different kinds of politics.

[1] This is a lightly edited transcript of Dani Rodrik's remarks at the conference held on March 27th and 28th, 2023 at The New School for Social Research.

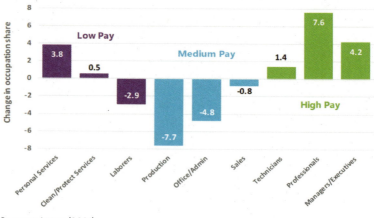

Figure 1: Employment Growth by Occupation and Annual Pay, 1980 to 2019

Source: Autor (2021)

When we think about the historical process of economic and political development, industrialization is, to some extent, shaping the development of the working class. The working class in turn becomes, after long periods of struggle, an organized labor movement that ultimately may underpin a kind of labor-based political movement and a party. If this happens, the labor party could drive all kinds of reforms and classical liberalism could either be transformed into explicitly social democracy or illiberal democracy, with a very strong redistributive bent. But at the root of this historical transformation, it is still labor getting organized through a process of industrialization, typically with workers gathered into factories in urban areas. When this process of industrialization is lacking, or when an economy has industrialized but is then subject to premature deindustrialization, the result is a disorganized petty informal sector of micro enterprises, self-employment, and the lack of development of a similar workers class. This is, in my opinion, likely to result in a kind of politics that is very different from what we have gotten in the advanced industrial countries of today. It is much more of a personalized and clientelistic type, which successful authoritarian populists, such as Orbán, Erdoğan, Modi, or Bolsonaro, are actually quite good at delivering in the form of very particular services to "the people", i.e. their electorate. While this is certainly not a deterministic process, I believe that one version of politics resulting from changes in the underlying economy is this authoritarian populism. Hence, these labor market trends, which have been driven by globalization, technological trends, and so forth, are making it much more difficult, or nearly impossible, to generate political regimes that we associate with the classical transformation in advanced countries. I want to explore in more detail how this is the case and what could be a democratic alternative to neo-illiberalism after the decline of the neoliberal regime.

Figure 2: Share of Pretax Income Going to the Middle Class in Select Countries, 1980–2021

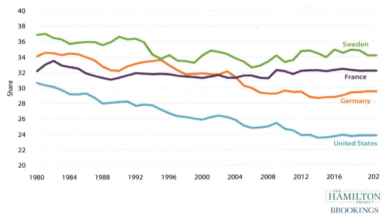

Note: Figure shows pretax income share going to the middle 30th-70th percentiles for each country.
Source: World Inequality Database (2021)

A good scenario for a post-neoliberal order would essentially consist of a step back from what is commonly called hyper-globalization, to allow greater domestic space and freedom for the reconstruction of national social contracts, where each country would remain freer than it has been in the recent past. Freer not just from extortive external regulations, but also at the intellectual and cognitive levels; freer to pursue their own national development models that might be appropriate in the specific context. The issue of industrial policies targeting good jobs has particular relevance for developing and developed countries alike. Indeed, in many ways, the disappearance of good jobs is at the heart of the rise of illiberalism and authoritarian populism, topics that are the concern of this project. In this regard, the well-known phenomenon of labor market polarization in most of the advanced countries is problematic, as it is hollowing out labor markets, with middle-skill-level jobs disappearing.

Furthermore, it is also true that in the most recent recovery workers at the very low end of the pay distribution have actually done quite well in the last couple of years compared to those in middle-class occupations. This squeeze of the middle class is reflected in a long-term trend, particularly acute in the United States. This squeeze has many implications, not only economic, with rising inequalities, but also social, even affecting health, to name one.

Figure 3: Manufacturing Trends in Various Countries

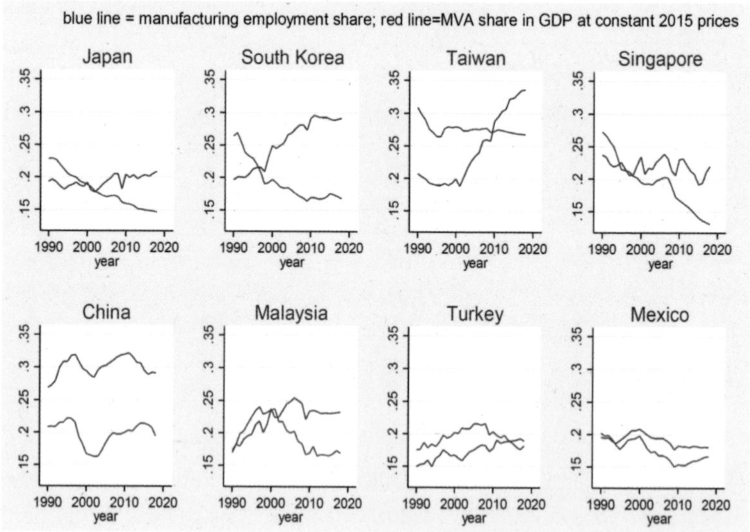

blue line = manufacturing employment share; red line=MVA share in GDP at constant 2015 prices

Source: De Vries et al., *The Economic Transformation Database* (ETD; 2021)

A different version of this dynamic is also playing out in developing countries. Specifically, the traditional pattern of structural change that governs countries' development is no longer working. The traditional pattern entailed a move from agriculture and informal activities to formal organized manufacturing, and, ultimately, to services, after higher levels of incomes were reached. Instead, what is observed today is very different. Even though people are still leaving the countryside and the agricultural sector, they are not being absorbed by the industrial and manufacturing sector, rather they are funneled into informal services in urban areas. What is observed is a phenomenon of premature deindustrialization in the low- and middle-income countries. Indeed, although these countries are still poor and hence earlier theories of development would have recommended industrialization in order to develop, formal organized manufacturing is actually *shedding labor*. Furthermore, even in some low-income countries where industrialization has gone ahead at a reasonable pace, an increasing dominance of informality within manufacturing is observed.

This country-wide polarity plays out increasingly within manufacturing itself. Hence, the challenge that the system confronts – and this again is common between low- and high-income countries – is that re-industrialization, i.e. trying to reignite domestic industrialization, is not going to solve this problem.

This can even be seen in those countries, such as Taiwan, South Korea, and to some extent Japan, which have been rather successful in maintaining high levels of manufacturing activity in terms of output and value-added at constant prices, as employment in manufacturing continued to shrink. South Korea is a particularly striking example of this. In South Korea, manufacturing output as a share of GDP at constant prices has actually continued to increase quite significantly since the 2000s. This is maybe the most illustrative case among countries that are trying to reindustrialize through, for instance, the CHIPS Act or re-shoring in the United States[2]. Just achieving half of this would look like a miracle in the United States in terms of re-industrialization. However, despite this re-industrialization, it is worth noting that manufacturing employment has nonetheless shrunk as a share of total employment. Hence, it seems unlikely that even re-industrialization would be able to reverse the trend of polarized employment. For this reason, the urgency

---

2   The CHIPS and Science Act, passed by the US Congress and signed into law by President Biden in 2022, allocates $280 billion in funding for research and manufacturing of semiconductors in the United States.

emerges for a new set of policies and the need for the post-neoliberal era to adapt, deal with this feature, and find a way forward to reverse these trends, through the creation of an increasing number of good jobs fitting the middle-skilled class.

To reach this goal, it is not enough to merely talk about re-industrialization. Rather, this discourse would need to be complemented by other interventions, such as investing in training and education, establishing standards, increasing the bargaining power of workers, setting higher minimum wages, and so forth. All of those are obviously important, but their implementation is not without complexities. Indeed, there is a tension between trying to enhance or mandate higher pay for workers at the lower-middle end of the skill distribution and the consequences for employment. This has been observed, for example, in a country like France, which has done rather well at keeping up the bottom of the labor market in terms of pay and standards. The cost has been very high youth unemployment, as people have trouble getting into the labor market at a young age. Thus, the only way this tension could be resolved is by complementing these policies of collective bargaining and standards and better labor market regulations with increasing the productivity of workers at the low and middle end of the skill distribution. This is, after all, really the domain of industrial policy. Indeed, it focuses on fostering innovation and appropriate structural change towards more productive activities.

Today, however, when talking about industrial policies and the variation of innovation policies, the tendency is to focus on manufacturing, supply chains, the green transition and global competitiveness. It is generally thought that jobs are going to be the by-product of these things, as in the case of the Inflation Reduction Act (IRA)[3] or the CHIPS Act in the US. But in fact there is no guarantee. Indeed, as mentioned earlier, even if the effort to revive manufacturing is to be successful, the benefit in terms of jobs creation will be rather meager, as nowadays jobs creation is principally shaped by the service industry. It follows that there emerges a

---

3   The IRA, signed by President Biden in August 2022, is a set of tax incentives and subsidies to stimulate and accelerate investments in the green transition.

new need to target industrial policies much more explicitly on good jobs. That also means that industrial policies will need to put as much emphasis on the demand side of labor markets – namely enhancing productivity in small and medium-sized enterprises that will be creating the bulk of jobs – in addition to enhancing the supply side of labor markets, through investment in skills and training that will have to focus much more on services rather than just manufacturing.

Let me now turn to briefly present some salient aspects of what this system might look like on three different levels. First, at the very local level, a set of local "industrial" policies would be needed, combining workforce development with business development to provide firms, especially smaller and medium-sized enterprises, with a portfolio of business services, an extension to services of the sort we normally think of as "agricultural extension" or "manufacturing extension". In this sense, there is a need to reorient the capabilities of these local cross-sectoral efforts to develop these business services, whether it's in terms of management training, access to platforms or technologies, access to land, or access to help with regulations, to name a few.

At the national level, it is necessary to invest much more directly in labor-friendly technologies. The tendency so far has been to take the direction of technological change as given. But of course, technological change is not given, rather it responds to incentives. One could imagine, for example, setting up an "ARPA-W," that is an ARPA (an Advanced Research Projects Agency) for workers that would allow investment in frontier technologies. This could provide frontline workers, say in long-term care or education or retail, with digital tools or other AI tools that actually enhance their performance and allow them to provide much more customized services to their customers, whether it is retail customers or long-term care patients. That would actually make this relationship much more productive while giving workers much more agency and autonomy in the way that they produce. In this sense, this ARPA, targeted at enhancing workers and their productivity, specifically and directly at the low and middle end of workers' skills, would resemble the current DARPA, concerning innovations in defense related areas, or the ARPA-E, the government agency focused on investing in green technology.

Finally, at the international level, there is the need to reverse our understanding of how the global economy and the domestic economy interact. Under hyper-globalization, domestic economies and societies are understood as being at the service of hyper-globalization. The main concern currently revolves around what is needed to be done to become more competitive globally. This question will have to be reversed. It becomes all important that we rearrange the system of international trade and finance and ask the question how global arrangements could best support cohesive and inclusive domestic economies, in a way that dates back to the spirit of the Bretton Woods regime, a regime where that support was very much the underlying concern. Moreover, it would be fundamental to include social safeguards clauses which protect domestic labor standards from erosion due to import competition.

Illiberal Political Economics after Neoliberalism

JESSICA PISANO
The New School

This section discusses concrete causal links between political economies of neoliberalism and political economies of illiberalism. It does so from a political scientist's point of view, reminding us that when it comes to vocabularies of analysis, political scientists and economists are often divided by a common language.

As a political scientist, I have found that a great deal of the scholarship about illiberalism misconstrues illiberalism's political origins, attributing the emergence and institutionalization of illiberal ideas mainly to anti-systemic masses or populist anger. Such accounts focus on emotions: the wells of discontent that carry populist leaders into office, the opportunistic manipulation of mass sentiment by those politicians. Yet while affect may account for some support for populist or illiberal leaders, much of the support we have seen to date for illiberal politicians is rooted in neoliberalism, but not in the ways one might think.

Coming to these questions as a political ethnographer, I have been interested in how economic change affects people's lives and how this impact translates into changes in local, national, and global politics. I have spent my career studying rural communities and company towns along national borders in Russia and Ukraine, where many people regularly have supported illiberal politicians.

These have included communities on each side of the Russia-Ukraine border, especially in and around the Ukrainian city of Kharkiv and Voronezh region in Russia[1], and in Ukraine's southwest, where Hungarian-speaking Ukrainians have been courted by Viktor Orbán's party since the turn of the millennium.

What I learned during decades of field research and in writing the books that came out of that research was that support for illiberal politicians was rarely programmatic.[2] Although people seemed to respond in ways that expressed programmatic support in opinion polls, in staged demonstrations, or at the ballot box, notwithstanding political illiberalism's heavy accent on cultural politics, I found that ideology in illiberalism is often epiphenomenal.

Importantly, political economies in illiberalism draw, but do not draw on, boundaries within the demos: while illiberalism *produces* something that looks like ethnonationalism, it often *starts* from an economic compact, a transactional politics.

This transactional politics should give us pause when we are tempted to see fascism, or proto-fascism, when we look at illiberalism – whether we're considering Putin or Orbán or Erdoğan, Modi, Bolsonaro, or Trump. Fascism depends on societal mobilization. Yet, with the possible exception of North Korea, there are no more closed ideological fields at the national level. Despite controls states may impose upon communication and exchange of information, people tend to find a way around these controls. For example, we see that today in wartime Russia, state

1   See, for example, my book *The Post-Soviet Potemkin Village: Politics and Property Rights in the Black Earth* (Cambridge University Press, 2007); or my article "From Iron Curtain to Golden Curtain: Remaking Identity in the European Union Borderlands," *East European Politics and Societies*, 23:2 (May 2009), pp. 266–290. https://doi.org/10.1177/0888325409333056

2   The following pages draw on the argument and findings of my book, *Staging Democracy: Political Performance in Ukraine, Russia, and Beyond* (Cornell University Press, 2022).

surveillance and the unavailability of certain social media platforms notwithstanding, people continue to find ways to access Telegram channels and other sources of information. People who want to learn from sources other than state media have options; whether they choose to do so is a different question.

Second, in illiberalism, politicians have played a role in the creation of political opacity, obscuring from view how politics are playing out at the local level. Efforts to limit free expression creates blind spots, not only for social actors but also for politicians themselves – including politicians with ambitions to charismatic forms of leadership.

One way to think about the resulting signaling problem is that in contemporary illiberal regimes, performances of democracy function less like an orchestra and more like a set of jazz combos: if at the start of the twenty-first century regimes that today are known as "illiberal" coordinated imitations of democracy from the capital cities following detailed plans specified in advance, today central authorities often outsource the task of manipulating publics to regional authorities. Those authorities draw on resources already at hand to organize improvised shows of support. For example, to optimize resources, illiberal politicians at the national level impose unfunded mandates on the regions, demanding electoral returns from regional leaders who need support from the center. To cope with these unfunded mandates, party agents use existing social institutions to deliver votes. Mobilization occurs not in response to ideological motivation, but rather because of the pressures delivered through these institutions.[3]

In such contexts, the center does not really know what is going on in peripheral areas: they do not know what the song sounds like out there. They know that there is an audience, and that they are getting the results that they want, but politicians at the center do not have a sense of people's programmatic desires or senses of affiliation. Therefore, although in certain cases we may observe formal similarities with fascist formations, we should be careful about assuming that the social foundations that could support fascist regimes are intact in illiberal regimes in the way that we would expect them to be.

3   I elaborate this metaphor at length in Chapters 4 and 5 of *Staging Democracy*.

Through my research, I also learned that people's support for illiberal politicians often was not a response to contemporary versions of the "iron rice bowl" that we see in the European right's co-optation of the post-war social welfare consensus, in which electorates express their appreciation for security and an improved standard of living by supporting certain politicians. Instead, what I found was that people very often supported illiberal politicians out of fear of material loss in a context characterized both by highly orchestrated political threats and the redefinition of public goods and the monetization of social benefits. Even supposed positive incentives that brought people out onto public squares or to the ballot box (including in demonstrations for hire or vote buying) for most people represented mitigation of greater financial loss and a hedge against risk for household economies, not a net gain.

It's important to note that in such contexts, economic anxiety intersects with and amplifies contemporary or historical experiences of bondage, occupation, theft, and exposure to police states. So, while I'm referring here to my findings in Eastern Europe, such processes and their reverberations transcend national boundaries.

This all leads to a situation in which an illiberalism that looks like statism or authoritarianism, or even some version of totalitarianism or fascism, depends on a bargain anchored in neoliberal precarity. That bargain is a contemporary version of Bayart's politique du ventre in which politicians, their agents, and their followers form rigidly hierarchical clientelist relationships that carve out constituencies within the demos.[4]

Until February 2022, the consequences of these arrangements and performances of support driven by a material bargain were visible largely in electoral outcomes. Today, we can see them playing out in the largest land war in Europe since 1945, in which participants and supporters in Russia are often motivated to sign up for, or silently tolerate, their country's imperial aggression by politicians leveraging consumer debt or the threat of loss of employment.

4   Jean-François Bayart, *L'Etat en Afrique: La Politique du Ventre* (Fayard, 1989).

Because of the elements of dramaturgy present in the contemporary politics of Moscow, the global seat of illiberalism, and because of the economic bargains at the heart of contemporary illiberalism, we cannot deduce from demonstrations of popular support for illiberal regimes any form of durable, genuine, or programmatic alignment with illiberal politicians. This can be a cause for hope. As we look forward to alternatives to illiberal orders, it behooves us not to forget that politicians such as Viktor Orbán in Hungary are dependent for their popularity in large part on the support and cooperation of liberal societies and their institutions: in Orbán's case, on various subsidies from the European Union, including for Hungary's transportation system.

Russia's war against Ukraine can also offer other insights, such as understanding the imbrication of Kremlin-based economic interests in the neoliberal experiment in Ukraine prior to the current expanded war. Nearly a decade ago, policymakers in Ukraine began a process of decentralization, devolving economic decision-making to communities, breaking up territorialized institutional structures that had been colonized by oligarchic interests. This move sought to strengthen sovereignty and broad societal unity while maintaining a form of capitalism. Now community-based work within an explicit framework of multiculturalism, such as the university-based volunteer networks I work with in the Ukrainian city Kharkiv, is playing a key role in the survival of democratic politics under literal physical attack. The model that this decentralized, community-based approach offers for the future of democratic politics is something that deserves further attention.[5]

---

5   The work of Ukrainian scholars points the way. See, for example, Oleksandra Keudel, *How Patronal Networks Shape Opportunities for Local Citizen Participation in a Hybrid Regime: A Comparative Analysis of Five Cities in Ukraine* (Ibidem Press, 2022).

Pursuing a Human Rights Economy

DARRICK HAMILTON
The New School

There is no better place to critically examine economics, authoritarianism, and democracy than The New School. In our history, we began essentially as an anti-fascist university. We have always combated economic oppression and pioneered new ways of understanding the economy and its social impacts and inequalities. And in our next iteration, I think we are ready and poised to understand politics and economics through identity group stratification – the ways we separate and divide people based on cursory identities and use those identities to distribute both economic and political power in a weaponized way.

So let me begin: the structures of our political economy go well beyond class and individual bigotry. As a matter of course, race and social identity in general are weaponized and linked to economic processes and outcomes. They are strategically used to generate hierarchy and propel systems of poverty, stratification, and persistent inequality, both within and across nation states.

It is naive not to recognize that essentially every policy and every structure in the US and the entire globe is racialized, and the impact of that racialization is by no means limited to Black people. Ignorance of both past and existing racial hierarchy under the guise of forward-looking race neutrality is what the sociologist Eduardo Bonilla-Silva accurately labels as "colorblind racism". Racism, sexism, and other "-isms" are not simply irrational prejudices, but long-standing leverage points and strategic mechanisms used for exploitation and extraction that have benefited some at the expense of others.

The framing of my discipline of economics as a science itself implies a purity devoid of politics, power, and tribalism, even though we constantly see those factors across space and throughout time and human history. Economic orthodoxy is based on a dogma: a faith that markets somehow are natural, transparent, efficient, non-discriminatory, and inevitable. This belief does not give enough credence to the political actions that form and codify markets in the first place.

The baseline concept of individuals or nation states as price takers does not adequately take into account power and capital, especially when we think about the inequities linked to identity group stratification, or international stratification across nations. As inequality continues to grow both within and across nations, we must move beyond the neoliberal framing that centers markets, personal responsibilities, and individual choices as the fair and just mechanisms of value and distribution. That framing lacks an adequate understanding of resource endowments, power, and distribution, and conveniently ignores the historical evolutions of how those distributions came to be in the first place.

Instead, we must move towards a new, more moral and fair political economy grounded in human rights and shared prosperity. That's why at the Institute on Race, Power and Political Economy, we are advancing the concept of inclusive economic rights: the promotion of human rights economies where economic rights become the cornerstone investment in our future and a necessary and inseparable component of human rights.[1]

It is important to understand the historical context in which the human rights framework emerged, in the wake of World War II and the dismantling of the fascist Nazi regime. In 1948, the United Nations General Assembly issued the landmark Universal Declaration of Human Rights,

---

1 The Institute on Race, Power and Political Economy at The New School, of which I am the founding director, was inaugurated in 2020.

in which human rights were recognized as universal and related to the human dignity of people and of nation states, with governments having the responsibility to deliver them.

The Universal Declaration introduced five basic categories of human rights: civil, political, social, cultural, and economic. We have forgotten that fifth one: economic. Although we have never fully extended these rights to all people, particularly those that are racially stigmatized, and those living in the Global South, there's nothing new or radical about an economic rights framework. An updated 21st-century iteration of economic rights would learn from the past about the failures of exclusion and unequal power. It would emphasize that the design, implementation, and management of economic rights need to be intentionally inclusive of all socio-identity groups and all nation states, particularly those that are most marginalized.

We think about wealth and resources as economic outcomes, but their true essence is a function of how they determine people's opportunities and economic and social positions, outcomes, and futures. For example, when we look at wealth disparity, mainstream economics blames it on poor individual financial choices and decision-making on the part of the borrowers of financial products. That framing is wrong – and so is the directional emphasis.

Wealth disparities instead are grounded in unequal and meager economic circumstances; they are not due to individual decision-making or deficient knowledge that constrains available choices. Disparities reflect how poor borrowers and poor nations have few financial options and are driven to obtain and use predatory financial services. As households and nation states with few assets and low incomes, they are compelled to turn to high cost, unconventional, alternative financial service products. They are generally aware that these products are predatory, but they do not have alternatives. These last resort debt traps result in indentured borrowers having to pay higher and higher interest rates, until they ultimately default on the original principal they borrowed, further depriving them of access to future credit. So, as we move away from more strict and obvious forms of oppression and exploitation, this use of finance is another way in which we indenture our nations and individuals.

Existing distribution of financial products is based on racialized, exploited, and extractive histories, so a rebalance of power with public intervention is necessary. The rhetorical illusion and elegance around words like "freedom" and "choice" obscures the narrow and specific notion of rights: not the economic rights of people, but the economic rights of property. This rhetoric ignores the immoral practices by which that property came to be distributed in the first place and the ongoing inequalities that maldistribution continues to perpetuate.

So, the neoliberal framing of our political economy naturalizes poverty and inequality by deeming it the result of unproductive or deficient behavior – that is, subpar outcomes are seen as resulting from personal choices by individuals, communities, or heads of states. That is the rationale for austerity policies. If behavioral modification, particularly with regard to human capital investments, is the central issue, why should we fund government and international agencies and programs? In the neoliberal framework, those efforts would at best misallocate resources to irresponsible individuals or nation states, and at worst create dependencies that further fuel that irresponsible behavior.

An inclusive economic rights frame turns all of this on its head by locating poverty and inequality as resulting from an absence of resources. Poverty and inequality are not rooted in bad individual choices and behavior, but instead come from policy choices that deny people the resources they need to live meaningful lives. One correction is for governments to end poverty directly by placing resources in the hands of people as a right.

Without resources, individuals are largely restricted from benefiting from economic markets, and instead are either at the mercy of charity or vulnerable to exploitative agents with resources in those markets. But in a human rights economy, governments have the fiduciary responsibility to provide the enabling goods and services that are critical for self-determination and people's productive capacities. Without these goods and services, individuals have limited agency to reap the rewards of their efforts or ingenuity. Our economic system is couched myopically in the value of self-interested accumulation, which leaves us vulnerable to greed and exploitation. Growth without human rights has become our explicit expression of economic well-being, but growth in isolation from economic rights fails to adequately capture the multiple dimensions of prosperity, including the full growth of human capabilities, morality, sustainability, and people's civic engagement.

We need measures of economic well-being and economic and international policies that center people and their living and natural environments as well as industrial policies that center people in the places they live. Without such a potent policy apparatus to provide pathways of economic security and self-determination for all people, white supremacy and the despotic political appeal for divisive and fascist leadership will remain, even in the face of overall economic growth. Governments have the fiduciary responsibility to reinvest in their most treasured resources: their people.

Markets and Democracy[1]

JOSEPH STIGLITZ
Columbia University

The natural place to begin to see what a post-neoliberal economy and society might look like is to identify the failures of the neoliberal agenda. We already know many of the economic failures of neoliberalism. These go beyond the economic – slower growth, shorter lifespan, greater inequality. The ways in which these interplay with the politics are pretty obvious. The growth of inequality has provided a fertile field for authoritarianism and illiberal ideas.

The kind of despair in de-industrialized places in the United States provides a reason for people to feel alienated from the current economic system. The social dimensions have been emphasized by sociologists talking about how these communities feel like they are left behind, not recognized, their voices not heard. All of these aspects of the failures of neoliberalism are fairly clear.

I want to begin with two points. One, for almost half a century economic theory has provided a critique of neoliberalism. Most of the doctrines that underlie neoliberalism were wrong even before neoliberalism

1   The research on which this paper is based was partially supported by the Hewlett Foundation. I am grateful to Andrea Gurwitt for editing.

became fashionable. Even the idea that free trade would be welfare enhancing was questionable. I wrote a paper showing that free trade in the absence of risk markets could make everybody in all societies worse off.[2] Similarly, capital market liberalization can be welfare decreasing.[3] So too, when you have endogenous technology, trade restrictions can help developing countries grow.[4] To repeat: the "perfect markets" theory behind neoliberalism had already been rejected at the very time when neoliberalism became fashionable. One has to understand that neoliberalism is not really a program based on economic theory, but a political agenda.

Now, when you recognize that it is a political agenda, it's useful to begin with the word neoliberalism itself: it's neo (new) and liberalism (free). The naming of things is interesting. One of the things governments have learned is to always name things the opposite of what they are. So, when you're talking about free, what does that mean? Everybody loves freedom, and therefore "opening up" sounds good. You're taking off the yoke that has kept you down. But of course, what we really should have understood was that it was freedom for some but not for others. As Isaiah Berlin pointed out, "Freedom for the wolves has often meant death to the sheep."[5]

Under neoliberalism, what was really going on was not a liberalization agenda; it was a "rewriting of the rules" agenda[6]: rewriting the rules in ways that advantage some groups and disadvantage others. Rewriting the rules is political – it is about power. The economic model that underlaid neoliberalism was a perfect and competitive equilibrium in which no one had power. So, neoliberalism began with a view that power doesn't exist.

[2] D. Newbery and J.E. Stiglitz, "Pareto Inferior Trade," *Review of Economic Studies*, 51(1), January 1984, pp. 1–12.

[3] Joseph E. Stiglitz, "Capital Market Liberalization, Globalization, and the IMF," in J.A. Ocampo and J.E. Stiglitz (eds), *Capital Market Liberalization and Development*, New York: Oxford University Press, 2008, pp. 76–100.

[4] Joseph E. Stiglitz and Bruce Greenwald, *Creating a Learning Society: A New Approach to Growth, Development, and Social Progress*, New York: Columbia University Press, 2014. Reader's Edition published 2015.

[5] Isaiah Berlin, *Four Essays on Liberty*, Oxford: Oxford University Press, 1969.

It began with that as a presumption, and then created centers of power. Financial liberalization led to the unfettered growth of the financial sector, which became a major center of power in the American economy.

Details in the rules matter, partly because even small changes to rules – transaction costs we might call them – redistribute power from one group to another. A lot of really small, subtle things have made a very big difference.

One of the societal changes that's been linked to the growth of "illiberalism" is a growing sense of insecurity. And the question, then, is: was that deepening insecurity collateral damage, as we were making the economy grow? Or was it actually an inherent part of the strategy? Consider again, for example, our financial sector. We created a system that got people *on the hook*, that essentially encouraged indebtedness (in the case of mortgages, even making interest tax deductible). Then we created a bankruptcy code that I've described in one of my books[7] as partial indebted servitude: those overly in debt just had to work to keep paying back the banks.

The changes in the rules of bankruptcy that led to these dire outcomes illustrate the importance of power and the deficiencies in our democracy: There was little public discussion of this change. But it had a very large effect on the distribution of wealth and power.

There are other economic and political (power) aspects to neoliberalism, but I want to talk very briefly about the moral overtone. I already mentioned "the freeing of all" that was associated with marketing neoliberalism. Milton Friedman wrote a book, *Capitalism and Freedom* (1962), to show not only that a neoliberal economic system was more efficient, but also that it led to greater freedom. Friedrich Hayek wrote *The Road to*

---

[6] For a more extensive discussion, see Joseph E. Stiglitz, with Nell Abernathy, Adam Hersh, Susan Holmberg, and Mike Konczal, *Rewriting the Rules of the American Economy: An Agenda for Growth and Shared Prosperity*, New York: Norton, 2015; and Joseph E. Stiglitz, with Carter Dougherty and The Foundation for European Progressive Studies, *Rewriting the Rules of the European Economy: An Agenda for Growth and Shared Prosperity*, New York: Norton, 2020.

[7] Joseph E. Stiglitz, *The Price of Inequality: How Today's Divided Society Endangers Our Future*, New York: Norton, 2012.

Serfdom (1944), in which he argued that if we have more collective action, we are on the road to serfdom. To the contrary, as I explain in my 2024 book, *The Road to Freedom: Economics and the Good Society*,[8] neoliberal, unfettered, capitalism has set us on the road to fascism. The implication is that we have to rethink the principles of a market economy.

Elements of a post-neoliberal economy

I want to turn now to discuss some of the elements of what I see as a post-neoliberal economy. I begin by emphasizing that modern economies are very large, complex, and have to be decentralized. I also want to challenge a view put forward by John Kenneth Galbraith that was very fashionable in the middle of the last century, which was of the importance of "countervailing power." Galbraith's view was that you must create large power groups to countervail existing powerful groups. I think that's part of the story. But we ought to be thinking about how we decentralize to make sure that there are no – or only minimal – centers of power. That is to say, there are always going to be groups that have power, more power than others, but we have to have much more decentralization, which will limit the power of any one person or group.

Another aspect of a well-functioning post-neoliberal society is the importance of *collective action*. If the government had not responded to the COVID-19 pandemic, we would all be at risk of the disease continuing. It was the government that provided the COVID-19 vaccines, and it was the government that kept our economy growing. So, we have just had a very dramatic example of the importance of collective action. Collective action is important in a wide variety of areas.

But even in the area of collective action we ought to think of decentralization. There's not just one form of collective action. Workers working together in unions is a form of collective action. Class action suits are a form of collective action. NGOs that try to represent the voices of people who have different perspectives are a form of collective

---

[8] Joseph E. Stiglitz, *The Road to Freedom: Economics and the Good Society*, New York: Norton, 2024.

action. So, I think a part of the post-neoliberal society/economy is a recognition of just how important collective action is and how many forms it can take.

Part of the strategy of the right has been to destroy, or at least weaken, collective action in every one of these areas. For instance, in contracts you can have arbitration clauses that give power to the corporations because the arbitrators, the judges, often have a relationship with the corporations. But then the Supreme Court ruled that there can't be collective action in arbitration. So businesses have succeeded in moving the adjudication of disputes out of the public arena – which is a core part of what ought to be in the domain of the "public" – into the private realm. And then they said that in that private sphere there can't be collective action. This is a concerted effort to weaken the scope of collective action.

The most important unit for collective action is our government, operating at all levels. And again, there's been a concerted effort to disempower the government, both by limiting its funds – that's what austerity is about – but also by denigrating it, making sure that high-quality people don't work there and limiting the domain of government learning-by-doing. If you don't have industrial policies, you're not going to learn how to do industrial policy. If you don't have a central bank, you don't know how to do central banking. We recognize now that we need central banks. Similarly, we need institutions that promote industrial policy. By limiting government resources and denigrating the public sector over the past 50 years, we've made the public sector weaker, and therefore made it more difficult to engage in collective action.

An important aspect of collective action is the socialization of risk. This goes back to the role of insecurity as creating a fertile field for demagogues and illiberal democracy. We socialize risk all the time. When the Silicon Valley Bank went down but its depositors were protected (beyond the level covered by deposit insurance), we socialized that risk. I think it was the right decision. But what is so interesting is that we have a neoliberal ideology that says, in effect, that we individuals should take care of ourselves and be free to do as we please, bearing the consequences. In the same way, banks should be free – but when banks need money, we *have* to bail them out. This ideology, which I've referred to as *ersatz capitalism*[9], with the privatization of gains but the socialization of losses, is not coherent; it is a reflection of power. I think there is scope for a more coherent post-neoliberal ideology, where we have to recognize that we can't bear a lot of risk individually. In some circumstances, we ought to socialize risk and we should do it in a systematic way, with a coherent set of principles.

Another area where collective action is really important is macroeconomics. Even the right wing has conceded that the market does not manage macroeconomic activity very well. They have conceded that we need macroeconomic stabilization policies. But then they formulate those policies in ways that limit the role of the state and weaken it. An example is central banks. It has become part of the mantra of modern monetary economics that central banks should be independent; but in many countries they are effectively run by the financial sector, so they're not only independent, they're also unrepresentative. And this is true even in countries in which those from the financial sector do not dominate the bank's governance. Even people who are not from the financial sector tend to be cognitively captured: they adopt Wall Street's view of the world, and, more specifically, what makes for a good economy and a good central bank.[10] The right argues, for instance, that they should operate according to simple rules (earlier it was monetarism, more recently it's inflation targeting); the intent was to deprive them of much discretion.

Wall Street believes in austerity, tying government's hands. When I was in the Clinton administration there was a proposal to have a balanced budget amendment. One of the big things we did was defeat that. But it was only by a margin of one or two votes. One could imagine where we would have been in the midst of the covid-19 crisis if that amendment had passed. And some countries have passed laws like that.

---

9   Joseph E. Stiglitz, *Freefall: America, Free Markets, and the Sinking of the World Economy*, New York: Norton, 2010.

10   See Joseph E. Stiglitz, "Central Banking in a Democratic Society," *De Economist* (Netherlands), 146(2), 1998, pp. 199–226. (Originally presented as the 1997 Tinbergen Lecture delivered in October 1997 at De Nederlandsche Bank, Amsterdam.)

A post-neoliberal macroeconomic policy

For the last few years, I have been working[11] on a vision for post-neoliberal macroeconomic policy. You can see the contrast between a neoliberal macro policy and what might be a post-neoliberal policy in the debate going on about how to respond to inflation. The Federal Reserve raised interest rates rapidly, without thinking about the turmoil to the financial system that might induce, either domestically or internationally. It was a no-brainer that it would cause turmoil. It has happened every time yield curves change quickly. Banks are engaged in maturity transformation, borrowing short-term, lending long, so if the cost of their funds goes up quickly and in an unanticipated way, they may well get into trouble.

But after the failure of several large regional banks, we discovered that even in their so-called stress tests, the Fed never tested what would happen if the interest rate changed dramatically. This is mind-boggling, undermining confidence in the Fed and its competence.

Even worse is the Fed's stated ambition to increase the unemployment rate. It is odd, to say the least, for a major public agency to say that its goal is to have an unemployment rate that is greater than 5%. And we know that if the overall unemployment rate is 5%, the minority youth unemployment rate is going to be over 20%. Now, the president of the Fed should say to the fiscal authorities, "This is going to be the unfortunate consequence of what I'm doing. It's beyond my remit to address such structural problems. You better do something about this. Let's make sure that that disparity in unemployment rates is reduced as I raise interest rates." But, while there was ample *talk* about the pain about to be inflicted (on workers), nary a word about that.

If we want an inclusive society, it's clear we need to build a post-neoliberal macroeconomic policy framework.

There are two final points I want to make. The first is a statement about the state of economic theory, and the second relates this to economic policy.

---

11 With support from the Hewlett Foundation.

A premise of all economic theory is that individuals' preferences, their behavior, who they are, their identity, is exogenous.[12] *But, in fact, the economy helps shape who we are*, and the economy, in turn, is shaped by economic policy, the rules of the economic game.[13] There is some evidence that if an individual becomes a banker, that person may wind up being more dishonest and more selfish, and if one studies to become an economist, one may become more selfish.[14]

The important point is that our socio-economic system shapes who we are and affects what kind of society we create. If more institutions are based on cooperation, we may be more likely to wind up with more cooperative people. And, in fact, the one part of our financial system that worked relatively well in the run-up to the 2008 crisis and post-2008, were our co-ops, which are called credit unions. And, for the most part, the credit unions in the United States actually did not engage in the very bad behavior that was so prevalent before the crisis, and after the crisis they continued to lend to small businesses. This is not a surprise, because they had a different ethos. As we go into a post-neoliberal economy, it is important for us to think about how our economic, political, and social system shapes people.

The final thing I want to say is about the standard way that economists approach many of the questions we are discussing today. They ask, what are the market failures? And then how do we correct the market failures? That approach gives priority to the market. Markets are the defaults. Markets are where we begin our analysis, and then we patch things up. I'm not sure that that's the right approach. It is a very useful approach, and I think one gets a lot of insights from it. Much of my work in public economics, both in the theory and the practice, has in fact been based on

12   See, e.g., Karla Hoff and Joseph E. Stiglitz, "Striving for Balance in Economics: Towards a Theory of the Social Determination of Behavior," *Journal of Economic Behavior and Organization*, 126 (Part B), 2016, pp. 25–57.

13   Stiglitz et al., 2015, *op. cit.*

14   For a discussion of some of the evidence, see Allison Demeritt, Karla Hoff, and Joseph E. Stiglitz, *The Other Invisible Hand: The Power of Culture to Promote or Stymie Progress*, New York: Columbia University Press, 2024.

this approach, so I don't want to criticize it too much. But, at the same time, I want to say that in many contexts, other, non-market, institutional arrangements have worked very well and one shouldn't necessarily give priority to markets. Moreover, as I have emphasized in other writings,[15] internally, even for-profit market enterprises do not use markets; they rely on other institutional arrangements for the allocation and management of resources. The flaws and limitations of markets are actually very deep. When we go beyond textbook economics and think about the actual functioning of the economy – the inequalities to which it contributes, the exploitation by the tobacco and food industries, the devastation to the environment, the opioid and financial crises, the depressions and recessions, and so forth, we see a world enmeshed with deep flaws. We have this mindset that while the market fails in all of these respects, the market based solely on for-profit firms maximizing shareholder value should still be our paradigm. I find that a bit paradoxical. We need to take a more open approach to institutional arrangements. We should ask ourselves: What institutional arrangements really work? And if they're not working, how do we reform them to make them work better? I acknowledge that designing institutions is really difficult. And what's particularly difficult is what we're calling for here, a change in the system, and that means changes in many of the pieces all at the same time.

In my two most recent books, *People, Power, and Profits: Progressive Capitalism for an Age of Discontent*[16] and *The Road to Freedom: Economics and the Good Society*[17], I have described the outlines of what such an economic system would look like, and in the latter book, I have described – contrary to the claim of Hayek[18] and Friedman[19] – that this alternative

---

15 See *The Selected Works of Joseph E. Stiglitz, Volume III: Rethinking Microeconomics*, Oxford: Oxford University Press, 2019.

16 Joseph E. Stiglitz, *People, Power, and Profits: Progressive Capitalism for an Age of Discontent*, New York: Norton, 2019.

17 Stiglitz, 2024, *op. cit.*

18 Friedrich A. Hayek, *The Road to Serfdom*, London: Routledge, 1944.

19 Milton Friedman, *Capitalism and Freedom*, Chicago: University of Chicago Press, 1962.

system is best both in promoting freedom and in supporting democracy. Indeed, I claim that neoliberalism has set us on the road to populism – to 21st century fascism.

Thus, our economic system cannot be separated from our social and political system – from what we are as individuals and as a society. More is at stake in the move away from neoliberalism than just economic efficiency. Moving away from neoliberalism is a critical step in moving towards a good, or at least better, society.

II

Drivers of
Neo-illiberalism

Why and How Precarious Workers Support Neo-Illiberalism

ROSANA
PINHEIRO-MACHADO
University College Dublin

Introduction

Dani Silva, 30, is an Uber driver who drives his car 12 hours a day and lives in one of the poor peripheral zones of a large Brazilian city. Like many other male platform drivers, Silva strikes up a conversation with his passengers as soon as they sit in his car, on topics ranging from poor road conditions and traffic to the political affairs of the country and rampant corruption. At times he also expresses his displeasure at the poor receiving social welfare benefits from the government and 'becoming lazy.' He voted for Bolsonaro in 2018 to 'change everything that is wrong', from moral values to urban violence. In 2022, as these 'wrong things' had not changed significantly enough to improve his life, he stuck with Bolsonaro, with the justification that 'at least he is better than the communists.' Silva is an actual research subject from a previous project of mine, but he is also the embodiment of ordinary people in Brazil – a platform-based gig worker who votes for the far right. Not an isolated case, his story is symptomatic of a wider process, particularly strong in the Global South, where a huge percentage of precarious workers – or low-income people just above the poverty line – support authoritarian politicians.

The worker who rejects a working-class identity or identifies with the upper classes is not a novel political phenomenon[1]. Yet, we need fresh lenses to understand how such a long-standing issue is being transformed in times of growing platformization. In this paper, I use statistical data and ethnographic evidence from three different research projects conducted over the last twenty-three years in Brazil. I focus on the reactionary political manifestation amidst labour precarity and, more specifically, on platform economy labour. I will discuss the Brazilian field site, but similar cases can be observed in other countries, especially in emerging economies from the Global South, like India and the Philippines. Recent scholarship on these countries has demonstrated that certain economic strata – that have been raised from poverty but remain in precarity – tend to vote for authoritarian leaders (Caspile, 2016; Heydarian, 2018; Jaffrelot, 2013; 2015; 2016; Kaur, 2014; Lero, 2023; Pinheiro-Machado and Scalco, 2020; Richmond, 2020). Building upon this finding, I have two aims in this paper. First, I examine how precarious workers in Brazil have developed political alignments with neo-illiberal worldviews. Second, and more important, I analyze how populist co-optation, combined with the algorithmic digital economy, has accelerated such an alignment with the far right.

To explore the nexus between labour precariousness and authoritarianism, this paper examines a specific segment of voters: low-income people above the poverty line, with unstable employment, in the informal economy, in debt, working in gig employment, in an increasingly platform-based economy. Representing a large part of the population pyramid in emerging economies, they are the product of 21st-century economic growth. Unlike developed countries' deteriorating working classes – the Brexiter or Trumpist 'left behind', 'declining middle,' or 'globalization loser' (Antonucci, Horvath, Kutiyski, and Krouwel, 2017; Caiani, Della Porta, and Wagemann, 2012; Kriesi, 2018; Goodwin and Heath, 2016) – these people have experienced some sort of upward mobility or material comfort, and have been labelled as the new/neo

---

1   This has been a foundational and well-documented debate in social sciences at least since the publishing of Marx and Engels' *The German Ideology* (1965 [1846]) and Marx's *The Eighteenth Brumaire* (1963 [1852]).

middle class or the New Class C. These sectors are consumer-driven and characterized by entrepreneurial and material aspirations. But they remain vulnerable to economic shocks. They experience a contradiction between an aspirational identity that despises any label that associates them with poverty, and a deep resentment of the fact that they do not get social benefits. They distrust the state and are frustrated by financial insecurity, everyday violence, and corruption.

In line with this volume's purpose, this paper seeks to raise awareness about the fact that to achieve a more nuanced diagnosis of the rise of global authoritarianism, debates about economic policy and performance for sustainable democracy should necessarily address these emerging sectors that represent an aspirational precariat in the Global South. These groups not only represent a large part of the global population, but also constitute that section of the demography where the far right has been gaining a major foothold. In order to advance our knowledge of neo-illiberalism in the 21st century, it is imperative to take precarity seriously.

Methodological note

The arguments raised here stem from three ethnographic research projects conducted over the last two decades (from 1999 onwards). These projects have all analyzed the political manifestations of economic activities in contexts of labour precarity in several countries from the Global South, especially Brazil. In my first research project (1999–2008, 2014)[2], I investigated aspirations, competition, and 'self-exploitation' in an informal street market in the city of Porto Alegre, Brazil (see Pinheiro-Machado, 2017). Afterwards, my research partner, Lucia Mury Scalco, and I conducted an investigation (2009–2018) into the political consequences of inclusion through consumption policies, and how this process impacted growing support for former president Jair Bolsonaro (president from 2019 to 2022) among low-income groups in Brazil (see Pinheiro-Machado and Scalco, 2020). Building upon the findings of

2   This research project was funded by The Wenner-Gren Foundation. Research for this project was also conducted in Paraguay and China.

these two long-term projects, my current project (2023–2027)[3] relies on ethnographic research and computational approaches to follow low-income people who are engaged in the digital economy and observe how they are impacted by social media influencers who have large numbers of followers on Instagram (more than 500,000) and post content about work, investments, and politics. This aims to investigate the nexus between labour precarity and authoritarian politics in Brazil, India, and the Philippines.

My research trajectory amidst highly individualistic and unregulated market settings led me to focus on the ambiguous and even reactionary dimension of neoliberal economic precarity – or what Verónica Gago (2017) calls 'neoliberalism from below'. The following sections argue that neoliberalism from below can easily turn into neo-illiberalism.

Precarious workers and neo-illiberalism in Brazil: An overview

This section examines various pieces of evidence that suggest a strong link between precarious workers and support of illiberal politics in Brazil. Before the election of Jair Bolsonaro in 2018, the progressive Workers' Party (PT), which ruled from 2003 to 2014, had secured its popularity among the poor through the provision of welfare social benefits and poverty reduction policies. However, in the last two presidential elections, in 2018 and 2022, populist Bolsonaro received more votes in all strata above the poverty line, including impoverished segments with household incomes between two and five times the income earned from minimum wages. This is called Class C, which is composed mostly (approximately 60%) of workers with unstable income who live with financial precarity.[4] A 2022 DataFolha survey showed that Bolsonaro had 51% of the votes in this segment (against Lula's 42%)[5]. Class C is the largest economic stratum, representing 95.6 million people out of a total population of 203 million

3   Funded by the European Research Grant, Consolidator Grant. Grant Number 101045738

4   Official data from Pesquisa de Orcamento Familiares, from The Brazilian Institute of Geography and Statistics, IBGE (2022).

5   Available at https://www1.folha.uol.com.br/mercado/2022/11/encolhendo-e-em-crise-classe-c-vira-motor-do-bolsonarismo.shtml

Brazilians. From an electoral point of view, Bolsonaro won in all states where Class C is larger than any other single segment.[6]

In 2019, a dataset from the Mapeo Institute, a privately owned database[7], monitored and tracked data from 2,513 public WhatsApp political groups in Brazil and mapped the most popular clusters of Bolsonaro's support. Beyond the expected clusters of Christian evangelicals and Catholics, and nationalists ('the patriots'), the third biggest cluster was less evident. This was composed of informal traders and sellers who used WhatsApp to sell merchandise and services, but also to spread political content. Following this lead, in 2021 we monitored[8] the social media performance of the hashtags #StayHome and #BrazilCannotStop on Twitter during the pandemic. The first hashtag was promoted by activists, public health advocates, and lockdown supporters. The second one was fostered by the Bolsonaro administration. In April 2020, the message that Brazil could not stop had higher traction on Twitter than lockdown support during the period of our observation. Our analysis of the accounts' bios revealed that Bolsonaro's hashtags were promoted by well-known wealthy businessmen as well as by micro-entrepreneurs. This is an example of how Bolsonaro had populist appeal and could drive home simple and direct messages to masses of informal workers and gig workers who could not conduct their businesses during the pandemic. In addition, Bolsonaro offered an unconditional cash transfer (*Auxilio Emergencial*) to informal workers, micro-entrepreneurs, and low-income people during the pandemic, which further ensured his popularity within this sector of the population.[9]

6 Data from the Consultancy Plano CDE (2022), which classified Class C as having an annual household income of R$ 2,030 to R$ 6,125. Available at https://www1.folha.uol.com.br/mercado/2022/11/encolhendo-e-em-crise-classe-c-vira-motor-do-bolsonarismo.shtml

7 The Mapeo Institute is a business owned by the computer scientist Diego Dorgam.

8 WorkPoliticsBIP Project (UCD/ERC) in partnership with LABIC, a data center at the Federal University of Espirito Santo (UFES), which is directed by Fabio Malini.

9 The Auxilio Emergencial disbursed during the pandemic was an initiative from civil society, in particular from a group that advocates for Universal Basic Income in Brazil. Bolsonaro initially rejected the idea, but ultimately accepted it, gaining popularity as a result.

Finally, on January 8, 2023, after Bolsonaro's defeat and Lula's victory in the tightest presidential election in Brazil's democratic history, Bolsonaro supporters invaded the headquarters of the Executive and Justice branches, as well as the National Congress in Brasilia, in a coup attempt that called for military intervention. Data from the Federal Prosecution Ministry[10] showed that 50% of the 1,149 people who were detained by the police on that day were people who received *Auxílio Emergencial*. In terms of demographics, 60% of protestors were men in the age range between 36 and 55 years. All in all, this paper draws attention to the fact that although Bolsonaro gets more votes as the indicators of education and income increase, diversified sociological data suggest that Class C – composed of informal workers and evangelicals – constitutes the ideological hardcore base of Bolsonarism (see also Barlach and Mendes, 2022).

The politics of Uberization

Lavinas (2017) points out that the first term of the Workers' Party (PT) administration (2003–2014) did not reduce the heavy tax burden on Brazilians nor did it break away from a neoliberal macroeconomic regime. Despite this, the PT era adopted redistribution policies that profoundly transformed Brazil. One of the main legacies of the PT's first term was raising 40 million people out of poverty and lifting them into the so-called new middle class or the New Class C, a phenomenon that promised a bright national future (Neri, 2013). Some analysts and scholars suggest that the amount of poverty reduction was overestimated by official data, but it is irrefutable that the lives of the poor significantly improved in the 2000s as a vast segment of the population gained access to the financial system and to mass consumption. In 2010, Brazil reached its peak economic growth rate at 7.5% GDP growth. The government's focus on 'inclusion through consumption' transformed millions of people into new consumers. One of the negative consequences of this market-oriented form of inclusion was to nullify the party's previous collective and participatory mobilization mechanisms. There is still an ongoing debate about the political impact

---

10   https://www.poder360.com.br/justica/metade-dos-presos-pelo-8-de-janeiro-receberam-auxilio-diz-mpf/

of such a national push on the poor. Yet, there seems to be a consensus that financialization and mass consumption inevitably bring about individualization and depoliticization.[11]

Brazil's economy resisted the global recession that began in 2007, but by 2014 the country entered a phase marked by deep economic decline. This process coincided with the beginning of a political crisis that was animated by far-right demonstrations and a massive media campaign against corruption within the PT. President Dilma Rousseff was impeached in 2016 when Brazil was facing a period distinguished by a political vacuum. We resumed our fieldwork in a low-income community in Porto Alegre at the end of that year. If our research interlocutors were developing new aspirations and enjoying a more comfortable life because of finance and consumption opportunities gained between 2009 and 2014, they were now heavily indebted and frustrated, particularly the males in the community. Teenage boys who represented the future of the country – the children of the new consumers – became young adults amidst a multidimensional crisis marked by financial insecurity, hardship, and unemployment. A few years before this, these young men were enjoying partying at funk balls and worried about buying Nike caps, but as they reached their 20s, they became conservative fathers, concerned with their obligations as breadwinners. It is worth mentioning that these groups did not experience significant upward mobility during the economic boom nor downward mobility during the crisis. Yet, the perception of loss within a short period of time was huge. It is also revealing that male voters attributed their previously attained new, better lives to their own efforts and merits, and not to PT's fiscal policies. Paradoxically, they attributed their subsequent failures to Lula, as leader of PT (see Pinheiro-Machado and Scalco, 2020).

Uber started its operations in Brazil in 2014, precisely during the beginning of the economic and political crisis. The corporation was the first ride-hailing platform to operate on a large scale in the country. For many of our male interlocutors, Uber became not only their main source

---

11   Although I do not disagree with that premise, depoliticization is a nuanced process, which occurs alongside new forms of politicization, and is more focused on female empowerment and de-subalternation (Pinheiro-Machado and Scalco, 2023).

of income, but also an opportunity to have a more decent job, which was perceived by them as a form of self-employment and entrepreneurship. Having had a life trajectory marked by racism, exclusion, and humiliation, entrepreneurship was a dignifying label for many of our interlocutors who had never had good jobs. For these men, the incentives for using the ride-hailing platforms were to buy a car, own their first property, and work in an air-conditioned environment. The negative side was having to work in isolation during long journeys and for 12–15-hour days. Platform workers have a labour-intensive routine marked by isolation, physical exhaustion, hunger, pressure, and mental suffering (Crouch, 2019; Grohmann et al., 2022; Ramos, 2023). Yet instead of complaining about being exploited by platform corporations, our interlocutors glorified their labour-intensive regimes through their individual mystification of hard work. This new perceived identity was built in stark contrast to that of their neighbours and old friends who qualified for and received social welfare benefits from the government or were supposedly linked to the local drug trafficking faction. This process quickly evolved to villainization of certain groups, considered *vagabudos*[12], meaning people who supposedly have easy income for being lazy or criminals (see Pinheiro-Machado and Scalco, 2020).

This far-right populism conquered the minds of low-income, adult, male workers. From 2016 onwards, with Brazil still in the middle of an economic and political crisis, it offered an extremist and discriminatory narrative that could be used against the poor and minorities who were taking government 'handouts', but could be encouraging at the individual level. Bolsonarism was a movement that self-identified as neoliberal at the economic level and conservative in cultural aspects. From an economic point of view, the movement that orbited around the candidate valued entrepreneurship and hyper-individualism as a route to success, and relied on a simplistic logic that the workers who work hard win, and that the state should not intervene at any level of economic life. So, when low-income, far-right supporters failed to make money, as they had been

12   The meaning of the word *vabagundo* is different from the English word vagabond, as explained in the text.

promised they would as by working hard, they turned to villainization of the poor to explain this failure.

One of the most perverse results of far-right radicalization was an increase in the stigmatization of poverty and the destruction of collective identities of low-income people who live in impoverished zones. Our research shows that precarious male workers bolstered their own identities by demonizing the poor. This process occurred alongside a strong conservative and even fundamentalist religious campaign, promoted especially by Christian evangelicals – the main base of Bolsonaro's support (Almeida, 2017). In this narrative, the hardworking family's breadwinner was threatened by a corrupt government, the lazy poor, and a perverted 'gender ideology'. Bolsonaro's campaign promise to ease access to firearms in Brazil made concrete all these economic and cultural dimensions: a gun would protect the breadwinner from bandits who might steal their few possessions: a cell phone or the car that could be used for work. At the symbolic level, a gun also represents masculinity and power, especially significant in times when there is perceived to be a feminist and LGBTQI+ 'insurgence'. A strongman in power could address this anxiety. All these factors together resemble a process of neo-illiberalism experienced from below, which is a combination of a demand for strong governing authority and weak state intervention.

After he was elected president, Bolsonaro maintained his support among low-income precarious workers through a continuous massive disinformation/misinformation campaign that reinforced the villainization of multiple enemies. As previously mentioned, precarious workers responded positively to Bolsonaro's anti-lockdown position. After the pandemic, in pro-Bolsonaro Instagram accounts I followed for research purposes, I witnessed investor influencers saying (obviously falsely) that the Brazilian economy had been growing steadily during the pandemic, even better than China's economy. For our research subjects, the reality of their lives – which were still in precarity and marked by hardship – was not enough to change their political views. Supporting the far right meant keeping the illusion that working hard in the gig economy would be enough to change their financial lives.

In the 2022 presidential campaign, we were monitoring platform workers' groups on social media. The qualitative research conducted by Ianaira Neves[13] on platform drivers and delivery workers revealed that their WhatsApp groups, which were supposed to provide support and avoid political content, were fed misinformation by workers who participated in the groups and supported the candidate. The messages suggested, for example, that Uber and other gig-work platforms would leave the country if Lula won. This activated fear and panic in these people, who had reinvented their professional identities after Brazil's boom in the platform economy.

In another data collection exercise, I followed key platform driver influencers on Instagram. These people do not particularly show their political views on their profiles. During the 2022 election, two influencers, with 11,100 and 71,200 followers respectively, asked their followers about their views on Lula's declaration that platforms should be regulated and that workers should get some sort of social protection. I mined the 831 replies to this post. The majority, composing 74% of the replies, rejected the idea of regulation, fiercely opposing labour rights. Lula had suggested that platform workers needed some type of protection against accidents. Yet the followers on Instagram were against the idea, saying that they did not need social protection or pensions since these benefits would increase the fares charged to riders. In an individualistic mode of thinking, the vast majority stated that 'good workers' would save money for accidents and retirement, implying that it is the individual's responsibility to save money for the future. More than the quantitative result, the qualitative analyses showed the most paradigmatic dimension of workers' neo-illiberalism, revealing passionate favourable answers supporting a crude form of free market ideology[14]. The fear of platforms abandoning Brazil was combined

13   This information was conveyed through personal communication and is part of an ongoing PhD thesis at Fundacao Getulio Vargas. Neves is a researcher affiliated with my project WorkPoliticsBIP.

14   Of course this is not homogenous and there is nuance reading between the lines; many comments posted on these Instagram accounts reveal support for revolt against large corporations and poor working conditions.

with an aspirational ideal – the permanent illusion that they would make money solely on the basis of working hard. In a country where 78.3% of families are in debt[15], these workers believed they would succeed financially by investing their money in cryptocurrency and other forms of investment.

How the digital economy is transforming the politics of informality

In this section, I move away from platform drivers to analyze the political implications of the digital economy. More specifically, I focus on retail sales on Instagram, a social network that had about 1.6 billion users worldwide in 2023. It is estimated that Brazil has 136 million users (equivalent to 70% of the population).[16] A report concluded that 93% of Instagram users[17] access the social media app at least once a day.[18] Selling goods and services on Instagram became a post-pandemic trend in Brazil, and this process is drastically changing the nature of the informal economy, and also having political impacts. In my current research project, I follow both low-income traders whose enterprises are online and the popular accounts these traders follow. These accounts are run by so-called social media influencers who share tips on how to run a business, invest, or keep motivated. Most of these influencers describe themselves as apolitical – but politics and the economic content is usually blurred (Riedl and Woolley, 2023) and support for populists appears indirectly.

It would not be accurate to argue that digital platforms are creating the phenomenon of neoliberalism from below. Verónica Gago's ethnographic

---

15 Confederação Nacional do Comércio de Bens, Serviços e Turismo (CNC): https://agenciabrasil.ebc.com.br/economia/noticia/2023-05/endividamento-atinge-783-das-familias-brasileiras-diz-cnc

16 See Datareportal, 2023: https://datareportal.com/essential-instagram-stats

17 See https://blog.opinionbox.com/pesquisa-instagram/#:~:text=O%20Brasil%20C3%A9%20o%20%C2%BA,menos%20uma%20vez%20por%20dia

18 All of these numbers come from reports conducted by a private consultancy and are included to provide an overview of the important presence of Instagram in Brazil.

study (2017) of one of the biggest street markets in Latin America, Salada Market in Buenos Aires in the 2000s, is a good example of the fact that this predated the arrival of digital platforms. Likewise, when I started fieldwork in an urban and informal street market in Porto Alegre in 1999, the neoliberal subjectivity was already there in a raw form of entrepreneurship: harsh competition among peers, rejection of unionism, and weak collective solidarity in favor of small groups for mutual help. My former interlocutors were street vendors who worked 15 hours a day, usually 7 days a week. Many of those workers rejected the identity of street vendors (*camelos*) and self-designed themselves as entrepreneurs or even bosses. The first sentence I heard in the field was 'welcome to the jungle'. In my five years following the street routine, I found that my key interlocutor's personal slogan 'If I need to be a slave, I prefer to be a slave of myself' was a largely shared worldview within the group.[19] The street vendors did not believe that they had rights as citizens because social protection had never covered them; their contact with the state was limited to violence inflicted by the police.

During the pandemic, masses of street vendors and micro-entrepreneurs perceived their businesses as being at risk. Migrating their operations to digital platforms like WhatsApp or Instagram was the alternative both in Brazil and worldwide. For my current research project, I started following my former interlocutors, the traders who were working on the streets in 1999. At the moment, I monitor 87 accounts of micro entrepreneurs who work in the same marketplace in the city of Porto Alegre. Many traders maintain their stands[20] but have majorly shifted their enterprises to Instagram. If the digital economy did not create neoliberalism from below, the longitudinal perspective allows me to argue that it is fostering and accelerating it, along with a political process that connects workers to a far-right network. The reasons that explain this process are various.

19   It is important to stress that the desire for autonomy and freedom was potentially positive in a country with a slavery past.

20   These are no longer in the streets, but are now in a low-income mall, still largely marked by informality.

First, as already mentioned, there was an ideological predisposition among these workers who gravitated towards a highly individualistic and competitive market logic. The competition that occurred on the streets is being replicated online, where these workers seek the attention of followers and clients. Traditionally, face-to-face competition implies rules around bargaining, honour, and reputation (Rabossi, 2004). Yet competition on social media platforms imposes new invisible rules, which are boosted by likes and followers in an algorithmic pyramidal infrastructure that puts permanent pressure on users.

Second, as is the case with platform drivers, working through apps became a more isolated activity executed on mobile devices. The traders are selling clothes or cell phone accessories not only during market hours but also late at night or at dawn, while their competitors sleep. A consequence of such a process is the romanticization of brutal and exhausting working routines (see Ramos, 2023). In addition, before things shifted to apps, despite several disputes that occurred on the streets, mutual help and local politics were part of everyday life. Traders had to face local police and authorities and fight for their right to stay on the street, which forged some dimensions of working-class identity. On social media, the processes of isolation and deterritorialization are detached from the local politics, which obliterates the last vestiges of street solidarity.

Third, and most important, my claim is that this context of online competition, inhumane labour experiences, and isolation led to far-right adhesion. The digital economy, therefore, potentially poses a threat to democracy, triggered by push and pull factors. The pull factors are everything I have already mentioned, such as the predisposition to a strong individualistic ideology that makes people seek influencers who are sympathetic to their goals and worldviews. The push factor is the algorithmic logic, the technological infrastructure that makes traders encounter the far right. In the context of Instagram retail selling, I hypothesize that the more traders there are online, the more inclined they are to support authoritarian populists. This assumption, however, must be put in context. It can be applied to certain platforms designed to foster alienation and competition as well as to labour contexts that have an ideological predisposition to support illiberalism. Feminist cooperatives of workers who use Instagram to sell food, for example, will likely be less impacted by the far-right ecosystem.

The network of traders I study falls into a digital trap. To grow online, unskilled digital traders need to follow skilled influencers. Such influencers push the idea of a wealthy and successful lifestyle that can be achieved with discipline and hard work. As one of the main influencers, who has 8 million followers, posted, 'There is no poverty that resists a work journey of 14 hours a day'. The traders follow a network of coaches who teach them how to use digital marketing tools to make money and get new followers. Investing coaches purport to teach workers how to save money, retire with Bitcoins, and make their first million. Religious leaders keep traders motivated to cultivate family love and not give up, as compensation will come. All these influencers are interconnected around the phenomenon of online business in Brazil, which attracts a large part of precarious sectors. By following the online accounts of 87 traders in Porto Alegre, I reached a network of 212 key influencers.[21] Researching their online political engagement, I found that at least 182 of them are pro-Bolsonaro, explicitly or implicitly campaigning for him. These people dominate the digital tools of online entrepreneurship. Therefore, low-income traders get trapped in a political network of influencers who support the far right. Amidst precarity and low earnings, many former street vendors now call themselves CEOs. They also join fraudulent drop shipping and pyramid multi-level marketing schemes in the hope of making their first million. Additionally, they also start following far-right politicians, which might indicate a process of political radicalization.[22]

Conclusion

Precarious low-income workers above the poverty line are vital to understanding the vitality of the new far right in the 21st century. Representing a large portion of the Global South's population, these groups face economic

---

21   Brazil is the country with the highest number of influencers in the world.

22   Since December 2021, when I started following the traders, I observed that they started following more far-right politicians in their business accounts. However, only the qualitative research will be able to assess the radicalization of such a process.

insecurity, indebtedness, and urban violence. Still, they are motivated to climb the social rungs through their individual efforts – rarely supported by state initiatives but instead by conservative religious groups. Economic precarity has ambiguous political implications. Many scholars (Hardt and Virno, 2009; Standing, 2011) have argued that anti-establishment dissatisfaction could potentially turn into revolt on both sides of the ideological spectrum. In Brazil, people's legitimate grievances and aspirations have been channelled by authoritarian populists who inflate their rage, fear and egos while systematically impinging upon their rights. Considering this context, this paper has drawn two major conclusions. First, economic precarity provides fertile ground for the germination of far-right ideas. Second, the platform economy further bolsters this trend in certain labour contexts.

Labour precarity fosters several reactive emotions that stem from economic vulnerability. At the same time, aspirations are built upon national propaganda that stimulates individual ventures with the illusion of the possibility of achieving high incomes. These complementary emotions are directly related to the ambiguous economic condition of those who are not poor but have not completed their ascent to the middle class. What I have observed in the field over these years is that one of the consequences of such a condition is a growing contempt for the poor and an identification with the upper strata. Furthermore, working in gig labour in the informal economy is usually a task carried out on an individual basis, aimed at making immediate earnings. This context is ideologically aligned with neoliberal principles of weak working-class identity and unionism, and a focus on strong competition, self-enterprising efforts, and individualism. However, I also found that in spite of such inhospitable conditions, the social nature of face-to-face labour encourages people to act and to voice their grievances collectively.

In this context, the digital economy can amplify the effects of such a trend. When international organizations analyze the impacts of platformization, they tend to stress two things. One is exploitation; another is the potential for connectivity, business expansion, and even formalization. In this paper, I draw attention to a largely ignored side of digital labour: its political consequences. My work shows that within labour contexts that are predisposed to neoliberal principles, working through platforms can boost adhesion to far-right politics. This occurs for a combination of reasons: online ventures are isolated in their nature, platforms produce a techno-politics based on an algorithmic rationality whose infrastructure is non-transparent and pyramidal (Bruno et al., 2019; Grohmann, 2020), and, finally, enterprising online has been a wild individual venture that demands long journeys of connectivity and exposure in an environment dominated by authoritarian populists. In addition, in the post-pandemic world, masses of new and unskilled entrepreneurs need to rely solely on digital coaches to learn how to grow online. These influencers sell not only their digital expertise but also their political views.

Finally, many analysts infer that this situation of deep economic precarity amidst a growing illusion of making money on the internet is unsustainable. However, I would draw attention to the fact that authoritarian populists have historically benefited from economic austerity and social crises. Therefore, the path to restrain the authoritarian turn and pursue democratic sustainability demands a robust and diversified set of policies focused on universal welfare benefits, employment promotion, reducing inequality, and providing public support for those who aim to access the world of the digital economy.

Acknowledgements

This paper was co-funded by the European Union (ERC, WorkPoliticsBIP, 101045738). However, views and opinions expressed are those of the author only and do not necessarily reflect those of the European Union or the European Research Council. Neither the European Union nor the granting authority can be held responsible for them.

References

Almeida, R. D. (2017). A onda quebrada-evangélicos e conservadorismo. *cadernos pagu*, p.e175001.

Antonucci, L., Horvath, L., Kutiyski, Y. and Krouwel, A. (2017). 'The malaise of the squeezed middle: Challenging the narrative of the 'left behind' Brexiter'. *Competition & Change 21*(3): 211–229.

Barlach, B. and Mendes, V. (2022). 'Discurso empreendedor da classe C mascara exclusão social e acena a Bolsonaro'. *Folha de Sao Paulo, Ilustrissima*, 22 September 2022.

Bruno, F. (2012). 'Contramanual para câmeras inteligentes: vigilância, tecnologia e percepção'. *Galáxia* (24): 47–63.

Caiani, M., Della Porta, D. and Wagemann, C. (2012). *Mobilizing on the extreme right: Germany, Italy, and the United States*. Oxford: Oxford University Press.

Casiple, R. (2016). 'The Duterte Presidency as a Phenomenon'. *Contemporary Southeast Asia: A Journal of International and Strategic Affairs 38*(2): 179–184.

Crouch, C. (2019). *Will the gig economy prevail?* London: Polity.

Della Porta, D. (2015). *Social movements in times of austerity: Bringing capitalism back into protest analysis*. London: Polity.

Ford, R. and Goodwin, M. (2014). Understanding UKIP: Identity, social change and the left behind. *The Political Quarterly* 85(3): 277–284.

Gago, V. (2017). *Neoliberalism from below: Popular pragmatics and baroque economies*. Durham: Duke University Press.

Goodwin, M. J. and Heath, O. (2016). 'The 2016 referendum, Brexit and the left behind: An aggregate-level analysis of the result'. *The Political Quarterly* 87(3): 323–332.

Grohmann, R. (2020). 'Plataformização do trabalho: entre a dataficação, a financeirização e a racionalidade neoliberal'. *Revista Eptic Online 22*(1).

Grohmann, R., Aquino, M. C., Rodrigues, A., Matos, É., Govari, C. and Amaral, A. (2022). 'Plataformas de fazendas de cliques: condições de trabalho, materialidades e formas de organização'. *Galáxia (São Paulo) 47*.

Hardt, M. and Virno, P. (2009). 'Multitude'. *The International Encyclopedia of Revolution and Protest*. Hoboken: Wiley-Blackwell.

Heydarian, R. J. (2018). *The Rise of Duterte: A Populist Revolt against Elite Democracy*. London: Palgrave Pivot.

Jaffrelot, C. (2013). 'Gujarat elections: The sub-text of Modi's "hattrick"—High tech populism and the "neo-middle class"'. *Studies in Indian Politics* 1(1): 79–95.

Jaffrelot, C. (2015). 'The class element in the 2014 Indian election and the BJP's success with special reference to the Hindi belt'. *Studies in Indian Politics* 3(1): 19–38.

Jaffrelot, C. (2016). 'Quota for Patels? The neo-middle-class syndrome and the (partial) return of caste politics in Gujarat'. *Studies in Indian Politics* 4(2): 218–232.

Kaur, R. (2014) 'The "emerging" middle class: Role in the 2014 general elections'. *Economic and Political Weekly* 49(26–27): 15–19.

Kriesi, H. (2018). 'Revisiting the populist challenge'. *Politologický časopis-Czech Journal of Political Science*, 25(1): 5–27.

Lavinas, L. (2017). *The Takeover of Social Policy by Financialization: The Brazilian Paradox*. London: Palgrave Macmillan.

Lero, C. (2023). 'Voting for Violence. The New Middle-Class and Authoritarian Populist Presidents in the Philippines and Brazil', in Pereira, A. (ed.) *Right-Wing Populism in Latin America and Beyond*. London: Routledge.

Marx, K. *The Eighteenth Brumaire of Louis Napoleon* [1852, 2nd ed. 1869]. New York: New World Paperbacks, 1963: 15.

Marx, K. and Engels, F. (1965 [1846]). *The German Ideology*. London: Lawrence & Wishart.

Neri, M. (2013). *A Nova Classe Média: O Lado Brilhante Da Base Da Pirâmide*. São Paulo, SP: Editora Saraiva.

Pinheiro-Machado, R. (2017). *Counterfeit itineraries in the Global South: The human consequences of piracy in China and Brazil*. London: Routledge.

Pinheiro-Machado, R. and Scalco, L. M. (2023). 'The right to shine: Poverty, consumption and (de) politicization in neoliberal Brazil'. *Journal of Consumer Culture*, 23(2): 312–330.

Pinheiro-Machado, R. and Scalco, L. M. (2020). 'From hope to hate: The rise of conservative subjectivity in Brazil'. HAU: *Journal of Ethnographic Theory* 10(1): 21–31.

Rabossi, F. (2004). Nas ruas de Ciudad del Este: vidas e vendas num mercado de fronteira. *Rio de Janeiro: Universidade Federal do Rio de Janeiro*.

Ramos, V. (2023). A gente é descartado e invisível: processo de trabalho, fome e insegurança alimentar em entregadores de comida in Curitiba. PhD Thesis, Department of Public Health, University of Sao Paulo.

Richmond, M. A. (2020). 'Narratives of crisis in the periphery of São Paulo: Place and political articulation during Brazil's rightward turn'. *Journal of Latin American Studies* 52(2): 241–267.

Riedl, M. J., Lukito, J. and Woolley, S. C. (2023). 'Political Influencers on Social Media: An Introduction'. *Social Media + Society* 9(2).

Standing, G. (2011). *The precariat: The new dangerous class.* London: Bloomsbury Academic.

Austerity: Why, What and How – Lessons from the UK's Failed Experiment

THIEMO
FETZER
Warwick University
& University of Bonn

Introduction

Let me tell you a little bit about my adult life as experienced through crises. In 2008, I moved to the UK and the first crisis hit and was very apparent. The global financial crisis affected many demographic groups and my own economic outlook. It also resulted in an excessively large PhD cohort at the London School of Economics (LSE) at the time, because many decided to postpone their entry to the job market. Many of these PhD students decided to study this crisis and what came from it – and I was one of them.

The global financial crisis was followed by the debt crisis, which was very prominent in Europe. It was followed by the refugee crisis, the austerity crisis, and the COVID-19 pandemic, which had dramatically different outcomes across countries, depending on the handling of the crisis. More recently, we now have the Ukraine war and the ensuing energy crisis.

This multitude of cascading crises is happening in the context of a climate crisis as an overarching challenge, and a global demographic imbalance, where our social system and our economic and social organizations face a demographic pyramid that does not promise a demographic dividend. Hence, many institutions (i.e., the monetary system, unified currency, the trading system) are challenged by something that mankind has not seen before. I see two extreme ways and many muddled ways that this can go.

It is in this context that my research on austerity has unfolded and continues to unfold. In particular, I have studied the origins and causes of austerity, as well as the consequences of austerity in the UK from a policy standpoint. Most recently, this work has been focused on the COVID-19 pandemic and its handling. I am currently working on an ambitious piece of work on the handling of the energy crisis that emerged from the war in Ukraine and the climate crisis more generally.

What crises have in common

Throughout my research, I was struck by the realization that there is something that connects it all, and this is something I came to realize last year while reconnecting with some of the readings from my youth, particularly those in psychology. The narratives behind the attacks on the democratic organization of society, particularly those coming from the political right, often tend to lean on the perception of government inaction, or its inability to deliver. For this reason, I believe that the empirical work many economists are doing to study and analyze the unintended consequences of policies is incredibly vital. This work allows us to understand why these unintended consequences exist in the first place. This type of loop is the common denominator that surrounds all of the above-mentioned crises. This is also what brings us here to this conference, to discuss the threats to liberal democracy and alternative social organizations that are being championed, such as illiberal forms of government and potential technologically augmented dictatorships or autocracies.

By living through and researching these crises, I have started looking for the commonalities they exhibit. We start with a shock, or a crisis, which is followed by a policy response that is often too little and too late, and has a specific signature depending on which party is in power (this is observed in particular in countries that possess a majoritarian two-party system, like the UK or the US). When they come from the political right, these policy responses are typically increasingly regressive. They are facilitating or encouraging outright fraud or leakage of public funds. In other words, they tend to benefit larger firms more than smaller firms by being explicitly anti-competitive and reinforcing monopsony power or the market power of specific firms. They further actively erode state capacity and, to some extent, further skew relative prices, particularly intergenerationally. Because policy responses tend to come with a specific ideology, and oftentimes they are too little and too late in a specific flavor, they produce unintended consequences, which require costly fixes of these policy errors. Because of the development of the media ecosystem, in particular the emergence of social media, the narratives around what these fixes should be oftentimes result in two very unappealing options: the extreme left interpretation and the extreme right interpretation.

There needs to be a policy response in order to fix policy errors, which automatically creates an industry of action. My experience over the last three years suggests that there is something common here that governments oftentimes simply cannot deliver. This is where the connection to austerity comes in as I think it has eroded said state capacity. The consequence of producing biased and politically shaped policies produces intentional or unintentional errors that will also need fixing. This contributes to an erosion of trust and a reduction of resilience on the part of citizens. This, in turn, will produce voluntary political disengagement by some groups and potentially result in erratic shifts in voter turnout that make the process of predicting political outcomes and navigating political engagement increasingly difficult. I argue that this volatility in voter turnout and the difficulty of predicting election results is one of the features of populism. It is about activating a voter pool that has chosen to be disengaged. A consequence of the erosion of trust is the rise of extreme individualism, which undermines our ability to overcome collective action problems. The minimum group size threshold, as economists would call it, that one needs might increase and make the collective action problem more complicated. Other consequences in the form of exit also exist: instead of exercising their voices, some may "exit" due to deaths of despair[1]

---

1   This concept was introduced by economists Anne Case and Angus Deaton in the context of the US in terms of drug overdose, suicide, alcoholism, etc.

or poor mental health, which ultimately puts us in a worse situation when the next crisis hits, triggering the same cycle.

I have observed policymaking in a range of countries, from the more democratic to the less democratic. I have engaged with policymakers, and many of them actually want to do evidence-based policymaking. But they do not seem to be able to do so, and I have a hypothesis about why this is the case. One thing that I have observed and find increasingly shocking is that a lot of the institutions that are archetypal institutions in rentier economies, such as heavily institutionally dualized labor markets, are seeping into Western market systems. The UK is actually adopting a lot of policies that are very similar to what you would see in the Middle East and North Africa, practices of bonded labor, which we know is shrinking the size of the pie, due to the inefficient allocation of workers to jobs. It is the rejection of individual freedom and a rejection of human relationships that could be built on an ethics of care and mutual respect.

All that raises the specter of some countries essentially importing a rentier economy and its institutions, just as I and many others are actively advocating for helping natural-resource rent-driven rentier economies cast off that institutional legacy or primal instinct and helping them build thriving economies. So, where are the rents if they do not have a natural resource origin? The answer may well be politics. Because every crisis provides short-term economic opportunities for money to be made by addressing the crisis. Yet even if this is done with the best intentions of all involved, within a highly polarized society that finds itself confronted with new and vulnerable technologies of mass communication, the invariable policy mistakes and errors that happen, intentionally or unintentionally, feed cycles of distrust, ultimately further eroding state capacity and resilience.

The energy crisis that we have seen in the wake of the Ukraine war and the different national policy responses to address it provide a unique opportunity to study and evaluate the quality of these policies across countries. This is essentially what I am currently working on and it brings together my own life experience, all of my past research through which I tried to illustrate the zero-sum failures of past interventions, and many more deep and very personal emotions.

In terms of the narratives around policy failures and inaction, there are typically three lines of argument: 1) the lack of data, 2) the lack of time, or 3) the lack of evidence. For each of these points, I believe we have a good understanding of why these barriers exist. On paper, all the right data exists, it may just not be available to those who can make best use of it from a societal perspective. In terms of time, typically, some crises are more predictable than other crises – the climate crisis, for instance, has been predicted for decades. In terms of the evidence, we know that this is heavily influenced by influence industries and the absence of experts, in particular the lack of incentives for experts to engage in the boring work of policymaking and working with government departments.

In the wake of the energy crisis, I systematically reached out to government entities across 165 local authorities in the UK as part of a randomized controlled trial. There was a lot of willingness on the part of these entities to engage with experts who proactively reached out. The problems of perceived inaction are often due to logistical issues. Around this framing and discussion of deliberative attacks on the government's response, which indeed exist, there are also a lot of logistical issues that impede effective, agile, and timely responses by the public sector, which is in charge of developing the menu of policies that politicians eventually evaluate. This is an important insight that we cannot ignore. Following my discussions with politicians and policymakers, it became clear to me that they *want* to listen to the evidence and to follow the signs, but very few are qualified or able to discern good quality research evidence from bad evidence. And again, these are normative terms. In general, and on average, designing policies for a country, for all citizens, is a highly complex task. Listening to the evidence is hard, especially when those who should be evaluating the evidence are not well-enough trained to tell good evidence from bad evidence, in terms of the quality. I think the research community can and should do more to offer their help and expertise, and our profession should get better at offering rewards for and recognition of this type of work.

What I have also noticed about policymaking is that with a lot of policies, the do-nothing scenario is often the counterfactual. That is "what is a specific policy proposal being evaluated against?" And obviously, if this is the framing that decision-makers use to approach a problem, then doing nothing in most instances, around a crisis, is not an option. If this is the only counterfactual the public is informed about and that has been considered, and what the evaluations were, for example through mandatory economic impact assessments, that are routine practice in the UK, then this is a big problem. The public needs to demand more and demand better to understand the menu of options being considered by decision-makers.

And last but not least, I must emphasize that there is a lack of skills across tiers of government, in particular low analytical capabilities, which means that centrally planned policies that require local data/information may not be well implemented. The reason that many of my freedom of information requests take a long time in most instances suggests that they simply do not know how to extract granular individual-level data and to anonymize it in a way that is not disclosive. Protecting the right to privacy of those whose data is being represented is important, but that obviously is a barrier for the research community. We would not want to be in a world where access to data is available only to some private sector players and some people in government. This is why, I expect, in not too long, that there will be a discussion of privacy as a policy parameter. Neither too much privacy nor too little is desirable, in my opinion.

The internal organization of government is also a central challenge, as governments and executive branches of ministries are organized in silos with limited inter-operation, communication, and cooperation. The Cabinets are organized in silos, which makes combining and merging data necessary to design good policy options really difficult. This brings us to the challenge of systems competition. In my experience working with governments, I have seen data rooms hosted in countries that I would describe as being quite far from Western notions of (representative) democracy. Based on my observations, concerns about data governance are very strongly founded. Looking forward, I believe this is where Western societies need to develop an alternative view and significantly up their game.

Austerity as a signature zero-sum policy

Austerity is a signature zero-sum policy that showcases many of the aforementioned issues. The specific design of the UK's implementation of austerity was very much informed by ideology, shaky cross-country empirical evidence, and cross-country regressions that I do not think uphold the quality standards of modern applied economics research. They would not stand up to scrutiny. And that, I think, is an important qualifier. Austerity, in particular how it was implemented in the UK, reflected the political realities of the time: old people turn out to vote while young people are disengaged (voluntarily or involuntarily, which is a different question). In terms of welfare reforms from 2010 onwards, we have seen a realignment of government spending along the age divide. Pension spendings have continuously increased, while spending that benefits younger generations (education) was drastically cut and increasingly privatized through higher tuition fees. This was followed by drastic cuts in welfare and protection spending, which mostly benefits the current working generation (see Figure 1). Those policies hit the poorest regions the hardest and exacerbated the existing divide. Those policies ticked all the boxes of what you would expect for the implementation of austerity. Looking at the data, it is consistent with what one would expect in a society that is organized by those who vote: those who turn out to vote get to have their say and influence policy.

Figure 1: Composition of Government Spending in GBP Per Capita in the UK (2000–2015)

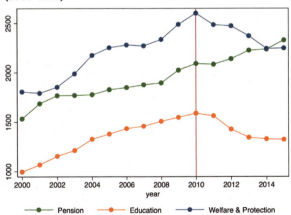

Source: Fetzer (2019)[2]

2   Fetzer, Thiemo, 2019. "Did Austerity Cause Brexit?" *American Economic Review*, 109(11): 3849–86.

Now, what were the effects of these austerity policies? I have written a paper that I think very cleanly separated and showcased how austerity basically caused Brexit through a range of mechanisms.[3] The most important mechanism is that due to austerity, sub-national politics in the UK evolved in a way that created the political pressures inside the Conservative party to put a referendum on the table in the first place. The vote that swung in favor of Brexit was quantified to around 10 percentage points, directly attributable to austerity, which is the signature of populist politics. The marginal voter was very much an accidental Brexiteer, someone who wanted to send a message, whereas the average pro-Brexit voter was one of those old signature demographic groups that we tend to associate with support for populism and nationalism. What we saw was the coalition bringing both of these groups of voters together during the campaign, which ultimately swung the result in their favor.

The bigger context is the economic challenges, and I argue that the welfare state as it was designed was just a Band-Aid for a larger, systemic problem. As seen in Figure 2, for low-skilled people, there has been a drastic decline in labor income that was stabilized by an expansion of benefit payments up to the point when austerity essentially put a halt to it. The cuts in the welfare state put the acceleration of benefit payments on hold, which resulted in a decline in gross incomes, eventually leading to polarization. This polarization is driven by many factors across the skill divide and can be observed across regions, age groups, skills groups, and ethnic groups, resulting in an increasing stratification of society.

The welfare state was a Band-Aid. Austerity ripped off that Band-Aid and Brexit was the consequence of it. And Brexit's legacy is the fact that the pain continues and the pain endures.

In a recent paper, I looked at the economic consequences of Brexit across regions.[4] Not only did austerity give rise to Brexit, but the empirical evidence also suggests that the alleged cure may be making matters worse. Brexit led to a culling of small and medium-sized enterprises, a collapse in trade relationships, and a more concentrated and hence less competitive market. This was followed by the COVID-19 pandemic, which created a

3   See Fetzer 2019, *ibid*.

4   See Fetzer, Thiemo and Wang, Shizhuo. 2020. "Measuring the Regional Economic Cost of Brexit: Evidence up to 2019". *CAGE*, Working paper no. 486.

shock in international science collaboration that affected researchers and their work. Overall, the cure seems to be worse than the disease and it is estimated that any benefits of Brexit will not appear before 2050. Since the vote, the narrative has been completely shifted around, and this is why I argue it is so important to study the unintended consequences of policies rigorously and carefully. This requires a careful distinction of quantitative as well as qualitative work. As argued earlier, policymakers cannot deny evidence, at least in (somewhat) liberal democracies such as the UK, and high-quality research that is hard evidence and sheds light on unintended consequences in near real time can inform the policymaking process and become an effective constraint.

Figure 2: Erosion of the Welfare State was the Equivalent of Removing a Band-Aid

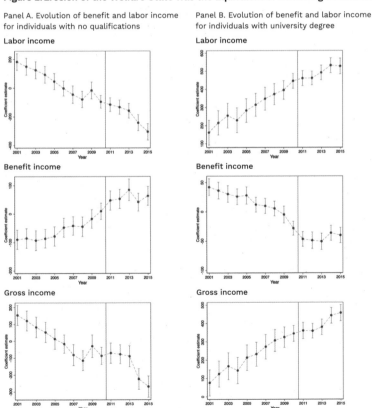

Panel A. Evolution of benefit and labor income for individuals with no qualifications

Panel B. Evolution of benefit and labor income for individuals with university degree

Source: Fetzer (2019)

With the change in the media landscape (i.e., professionalization of data journalism), informed research can constrain policymaking and serve as – and also reinvent – checks and balances. I am hoping to make a contribution here over the coming months and years.

Finally, it is crucial to remember that austerity itself is not a policy but rather a general reduction in government spending and that there are many ways of implementing it. Curiously enough, many of the policies that have been lumped together under the austerity bundle can be rationalized (i.e., in the context of fighting climate change). One must therefore not be blindsided by austerity's big label and understand that the devil is in the detail. It is the duty of the economics profession to make sure it equips its graduates with the skillset to do the right thing, know where to find which literature to read, which data to use, and how to analyze it – skills many policymakers of our time lack.

I would like to end on a note that reflects my ongoing struggle. I do not think humans are genuinely bad. We are all shaped by our own experiences and preconceptions and many more things. How we read evidence and interpret what is happening in the world is shaped by many factors, and the last twenty years have seen drastic changes to how information is produced and how it is consumed. We should not lose sight of this as this may create noise. I am a firm believer that the world would be better with more dialogue, more data, and more hard research as this can produce less polarized debates. We should speak more with each other, rather than about each other. Researchers need to do more to actively explain their work. And I also sense that society may need to face some debates that it has actively shied away from for a long time. Consensual approaches to policymaking empowered or constrained by rigorous evidence, though, may require giving up some of the spoils that come with political power, i.e., control over political rents, that may mostly be information rents. Humanity is facing an existential crisis and we simply cannot afford to succumb to narcissism. Strengthening and re-building state capacity is vital. And since the Global North is ultimately asking the Global South not to follow its specific development path – owing to the carbon footprint that it entails – it is vital that the Global North pushes ahead. The onus is on us.

The Enduring Social and Economic Consequences of the China Trade Shock

DAVID
AUTOR
MIT

Introduction

This paper will discuss the enduring social and economic consequences of the China trade shock. It will then turn to the political entailments that have followed and where they may take us.

China's rise as a world manufacturing power

China's historic rise as a world manufacturing power is illustrated by Figure 1, where its share of world manufacturing exports increased from just above 0% in 1985 to nearly 20% in 2013, and it has risen subsequently. The surprise in this figure is not the large share of world manufacturing China has now captured; this is to be expected given China's enormous physical and human capital resources. Rather, the surprise is the speed at which China went from about 2% of world manufacturing in 1990 to approximately one-fifth of all manufacturing today. No such rapid increase had ever been observed before in such a brief period of time.

China's historic rise as a manufacturing power is rooted in substantial part in internal developments within China itself. In the late 1980s, Deng Xiaoping, Chairman of the PRC, commenced market reforms and opening to world trade that, among other things, enabled the flow of foreign direct investment into China and ultimately prompted the movement of hundreds of millions of people out of low-productivity agriculture in the Chinese countryside into highly productive export processing zones (see Figure 2). This radical change, and China's entry into the world economy, followed decades of continual political and economic upheaval under Mao Zedong. This change did not emanate primarily from US foreign policy but rather from China's own internal developments.

Figure 1: Shares of World Manufacturing Exports, 1985–2013

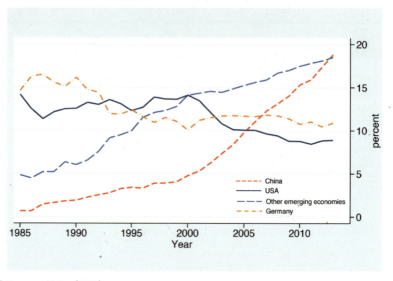

Source: Autor (2017)

This radical change can be observed in the landscape of Chinese cities. Shenzhen, which was a small fishing settlement in 1970, is today a vibrant city with skyscrapers inhabited by more than 12 million people. Over the past 50 years, Shenzhen's population has exploded, largely due to the growth of manufacturing jobs: most of the world's consumer appliances are assembled in the city's factories. China's rise as a manufacturing superpower, illustrated by Shenzhen's example, can be understood in three acts: (1) initiation from 1991 to 2000; (2) intensification from 2001 to 2010; and (3) stabilization from 2011 to 2018 (see Figure 3).

Figure 2: Special Economic Zones (SEZs) in China

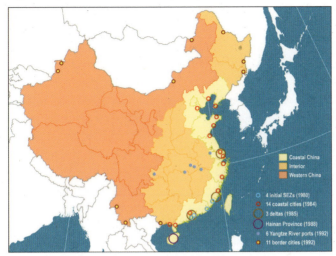

Source: Rodrigue (2020)

Figure 3: China's Import Penetration in the US Market, 1991–2018

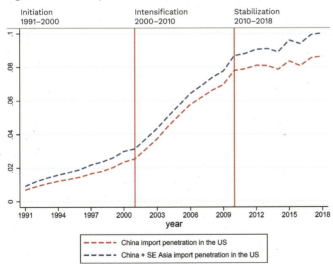

Note: Import penetration is defined as the ratio of US imports of manufactured goods to US domestic absorption (defined as gross output plus imports minus exports).
Source: Autor, Dorn, and Hanson (2021)

China's initiation is characterized by the internal reforms that enabled it to enter the modern manufacturing trading system. This period is illustrated by a slow but steady uptake of manufacturing exports to the US. The intensification period begins as China is granted Permanent Normal Trade Relations with the US in 2000, followed by China joining the World Trade Organization (WTO) in 2001. Starting then and for the following decade, China's import penetration in the US (i.e., its production of manufacturing goods consumed in the US) increased explosively (from 3% to 8%). After 2010, China's manufacturing entered a stabilization period during which its export growth slowed and its productivity boom decelerated. This period is characterized by a large-scale re-allocation of investment and a focus away from free enterprise and towards state owned enterprises (SOEs). The primary China trade shock, as many understand, is characterized by a 10-year period that is already behind us. The ensuing decade of relative stasis provides an opportunity to separate the longer run consequences of the China trade shock from its short-term impacts visible while it was ongoing.

The impact on the US and other countries

It can be argued that China's growth over the last three decades has created the modern world's middle class. Not only has it brought half a billion Chinese citizens out of poverty, it has also created prosperity in Central and South America, and spurred renewed investment in Sub-Saharan Africa, which was largely neglected by the West. Some may argue that this was not a benevolent investment, but when has Western investment ever been? On the plus side, these investments might also have caused the US and other countries to start competing for the attention of Sub-Saharan African governments. In his 2022 *American Affairs* article, David Grewal argues that one could imagine a different future in which the West had cultivated more democratic and westerly countries, arguing that there might be a third alternative to the "China's rise versus not China's rise" debate. Nonetheless, it is hard to overstate the importance of how much prosperity China's rise has brought to the rest of the world.

The case for free trade

David Ricardo, the classical British Portuguese economist, observed and coined the phrase "comparative advantage." His insight was that trade allows countries to specialize in the goods in which they are relatively more productive. This means that rich and poor countries can both benefit from trading amongst themselves and with one another, even if rich countries have an absolute productivity advantage in everything they produce. In stark terms, free trade among consenting nations has the potential to raise GDP in all of them. In a *Journal of Economic Literature* article in 1997, Paul Krugman put this forcefully: "If economists ruled the world, there'd be no need for a World Trade Organization. The economist's case for free trade is essentially a unilateral case: a country serves its own interest by pursuing free trade regardless of what other countries may do."

Trade creates winners and losers, however. What is true for the welfare of a country in the aggregate does not necessarily apply for all the citizens in that country. Trade is redistributive. It has diffuse benefits and concentrated costs, both in theory and in practice; without compensatory policies, trade will grow the size of the pie and shrink some slices in absolute terms. Hence, dramatic changes in terms of trade are inseparable from redistributive consequences. Arguing that countries should simply engage in trading any goods with any country that is willing to trade, without attending to the domestic impacts, neglects the redistributive consequences of such trade.

As Krugman and Obstfeld (2008) argue, "owners of a country's abundant factors gain from trade, but owners of scarce factors lose... this means that international trade tends to make low-skilled workers in the United States worse off – not just temporarily, but on a sustained basis." By implication, trade with high-productivity, low-wage countries such as China is particularly likely to reduce the earning power of manufacturing workers in competing industries, and especially among non-college workers who do most of the manufacturing production. One component of that impact can be seen in the falling US manufacturing employment share (see Figure 4).

Manufacturing's share of employment began its decline within a few years of the close of the Second World War, and a further acceleration of that decline can be observed around the time China joined the WTO in 2001. A substantial share of that recent decline, at least 40%, can be confidently attributed to changes in trade.

Figure 4: The Falling US Manufacturing Employment Share, 1979–2019

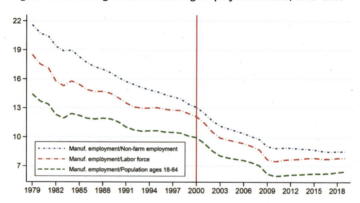

Note: US manufacturing employment shares of total employment, labor force, and working-age population.
Source: Autor (2022)

Figure 5: US Manufacturing Employment, 1940–2023

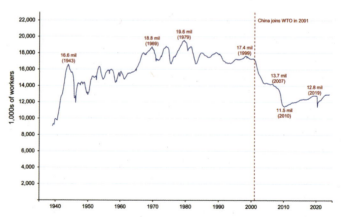

Source: Data from St. Louis Federal Reserve Economic Data, All Employees, Manufacturing

Turning from the share to the count of manufacturing employment tells a more dramatic story. The high-water mark of us manufacturing employment was in 1979, when there were 19.6 million us manufacturing workers (see Figure 5). Over the following two decades, this number slowly declined to 17.4 million – about a 100,000 net reduction in manufacturing employment per year over two decades. Following that period, manufacturing employment fell much more rapidly – declining by a further 3.7 million over the course of 7 years – and fell even further during the Great Recession (although this last decline is not due of trade per se). After the financial crisis, manufacturing employment had something of a rebound, with the exception of the Covid-19 pandemic, and went back to levels seen before the global financial crisis. The drastic dip between 2000 and 2007 is unlike anything the us has seen since the Great Depression. While the long sweep of technological change has played a leading role in manufacturing's secular employment decline, this slow-moving process cannot explain the precipitous fall after 2000.

Concentrated impact on manufacturing areas

In relative terms, one might think that 3.5 million manufacturing jobs might not be strongly felt in an economy of 150 million workers. Evenly distributed across 3,150 counties, for example, it would represent approximately 1,100 workers per county nationwide, which is not necessarily a large number. But manufacturing jobs are highly geographically concentrated (see Figure 6), and typically in just a few activities in each locale. Consequently, the loss of manufacturing jobs often knocks out central economic pillars in affected locations. Not only are manufacturing workers directly affected, but so are the manufacturing-intensive communities in which they are housed. Examples would include those specialized in the labor-intensive goods in which China gained comparative advantage; places making furniture, games and toys, sporting and athletic goods, plastic products, electronic components, and motor vehicle parts.

The effects of the trade shock were especially strongly felt in small localities. This has been observed, for example, in West Hickory, North Carolina, the former self-proclaimed "furniture capital of the world," where the percentage of working age adults in manufacturing fell from 34.1% in 1990 to 15% in 2016 (see Figure 7). During that same period, government transfers per capita to residents rose from $3,400 to $9,600. Another example is Martinsville, Virginia, the former self-proclaimed "sweatshirt capital of the world," where manufacturing employment fell by two thirds, the fraction of adults working fell by a quarter, and government transfers per capita increased by more than 200%.

Figure 6: Concentrated Impact of China Trade Shock, 1990–2007

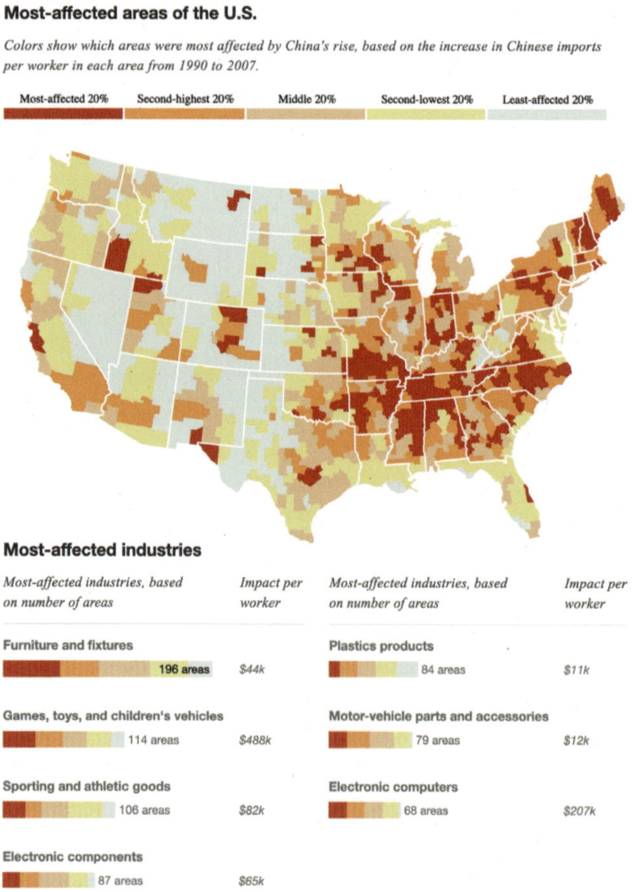

Most-affected areas of the U.S.

Colors show which areas were most affected by China's rise, based on the increase in Chinese imports per worker in each area from 1990 to 2007.

Most-affected 20% | Second-highest 20% | Middle 20% | Second-lowest 20% | Least-affected 20%

Most-affected industries

Most-affected industries, based on number of areas	Impact per worker	Most-affected industries, based on number of areas	Impact per worker
Furniture and fixtures — 196 areas	$44k	Plastics products — 84 areas	$11k
Games, toys, and children's vehicles — 114 areas	$488k	Motor-vehicle parts and accessories — 79 areas	$12k
Sporting and athletic goods — 106 areas	$82k	Electronic computers — 68 areas	$207k
Electronic components — 87 areas	$65k		

Source: Van Dam and Ma (2016), data from Autor, Dorn, and Hanson (2016a)

Figure 7: The Cases of West Hickory, North Carolina and Martinsville, Virginia

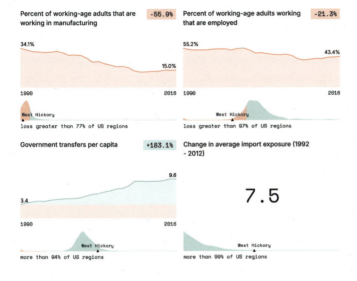

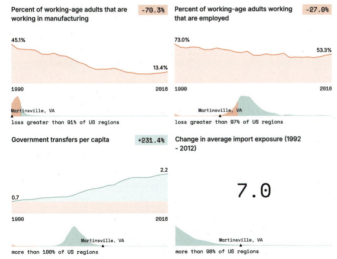

Source: Autor, Dorn, and Hanson (2016b), data from Autor, Dorn, and Hanson (2016a)

Empirical evidence of the China trade shock

Rigorous evidence is presented in Autor, Dorn, and Hanson (2013), which studied the effect of the China trade shock on manufacturing employment. That paper finds that every $1,000 intensification of trade per capita reduces manufacturing employment by about a percentage point (see Figure 8). This reduction is substantial, given that only 12% of the working-age adult population was employed in manufacturing in 1990.

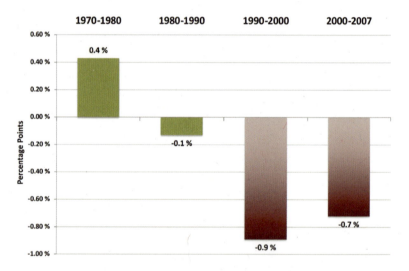

Figure 8: Effects of $1,000 China Trade Shock on Manufacturing Employment per US Adult by Decade, 1970–2007

Note: Change in manufacturing employment, as a percentage of the working age population, that is attributable to a $1,000 per worker increase in imports from China.
Source: Data from Autor, Dorn, and Hanson (2013)

Trade lowers prices by displacing higher-cost domestic production and replacing it with lower-cost foreign production. By implication, these cost savings are inseparable from the displacement of workers who produce these goods domestically. Using data from the UK, a paper by David Dorn and Peter Levell verifies this implication. UK industries like shoes, garments, appliances, and jewelry had outsized exposure, resulting in sizable price declines (for example, 40% for garments). Industries that were less exposed to imports (e.g., fishery, cars, and newspapers) also had smaller price declines. As predicted by theory and common sense, most of the sectors that had large price declines also had sharp employment declines (e.g., shoes and garments, jewelry, furniture, and appliances, but not so much in fish products). This is generally beneficial for consumers, a large number of whom receive small but meaningful cost savings.

The question that follows – which cannot be answered by theory – is what happens to workers who are displaced from their jobs and to the manufacturing-intensive communities in which they live. And the answer to this question, established by a large body of work focusing on displaced US workers, is that most of this displacement has been accompanied by a rise in unemployment and non-employment rather than an increase in non-manufacturing employment (see Figure 9).

Figure 9: Loss of Manufacturing Employment Not Primarily Offset by Rising Non-Manufacturing Employment, 1990–2007

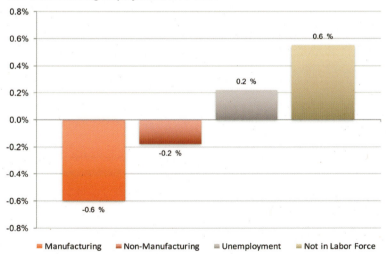

Note: Change in the share of population in each employment category that is attributable to a $1,000 per-worker increase in imports from China during 1990–2007.
Source: Data from Autor, Dorn, and Hanson (2013)

Not surprisingly, college-educated workers were relatively more successful at relocating out of manufacturing and into other activities, with a slight rise in unemployment (see Figure 10). Conversely, among workers with no college education, a strong decline in manufacturing employment can be observed, alongside a fall in non-manufacturing employment and a very large rise in non-participation in the workforce. Thus, although the relocation out of import-competing sectors was in some sense an inevitable result of rising import penetration, the unhappy surprise is how unsuccessful the ensuing adjustment process was: a substantial fraction of displaced workers did not find alternative employment.

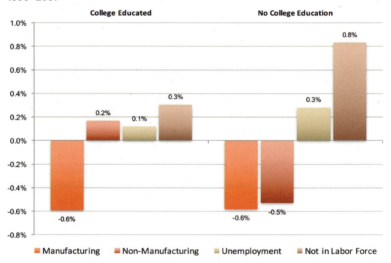

Figure 10: Effects are More Pronounced for Adults with No College Education, 1990–2007

Note: Change in the share of population in each employment category that is attributable to a $1,000 per-worker increase in imports from China during 1990–2007.
Source: Data from Autor, Dorn, and Hanson (2013)

These consequences extend beyond the realm of employment. As William Julius Wilson stated in his 1996 book *When Work Disappears*, "A neighborhood in which people are poor but employed is different from a neighborhood in which people are poor and jobless. Many of today's problems in the inner-city ghetto neighborhoods – crime, family dissolution, welfare, low levels of social organization, and so on – are fundamentally a consequence of the disappearance of work." Research by Autor, Dorn, and Hanson (2019) looks at what happens when work disappears. Analyzing the China trade shock, the authors document that it had larger direct effects on the employment and the earnings of low-educated men than on low-educated women, despite the presence of many women in labor-intensive manufacturing, particularly in textiles and assembly (see Figure 11).

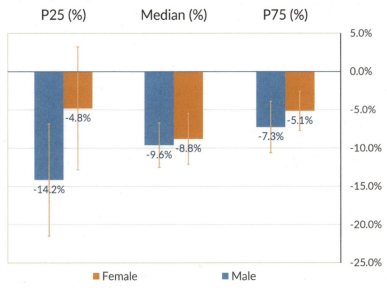

Figure 11: Trade Shock Leads to Drop in Lower Tail of Earnings Distribution, Especially Among Men, 1990–2014

Source: Data from Autor, Dorn, and Hanson (2019)

The trade shock led to a particularly steep drop in the lower quartile of male earnings. From a traditional economic perspective, this was potentially a destabilizing change, considering that traditional family structures are frequently built on a foundation of relatively high-earning male full-time workers, while women are less likely to be employed full-time. Following the trade shock, marriage rates among young women in areas most affected by the trade shock saw a sharp decline (see Figure 12).

The fraction of young women living with a spouse or partner fell, and the fraction living in some other arrangement rose by a corresponding amount. While fertility was not substantially affected, the fraction of children living in poverty, and the share living in single-parent and grandparent-headed households, rose measurably.

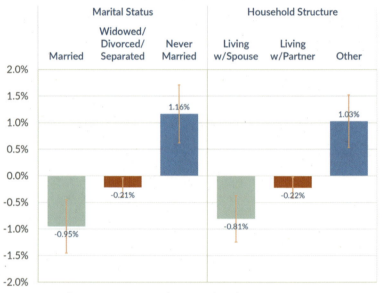

Figure 12: Trade Shock Leads to a Fall in Fraction of Women Ages 18–39 who are Married or Living with a Spouse/Partner, 1990–2014

Source: Data from Autor, Dorn, and Hanson (2019)

In summary, the change in earnings resulting from the trade shock arguably catalyzed a change in marital arrangements that subsequently changed children's living circumstances.

Other evidence suggests the potential for further social dysfunction (see Figure 13). Premature mortality due to drug and alcohol poisoning rose in heavily trade-impacted areas. This phenomenon, which the economists Anne Case and Angus Deaton have coined "deaths of despair," coincided with a rise in deaths due to HIV (often related to IV drug use) and homicide, especially among males.

These results point to the fact that work not only provides earnings, it provides structure, identity, self-esteem, friendships, and a foundation on which other social arrangements rest. When work declines, many of the edifices that stand on it tend to crumble. As Krugman wrote in the *New York Times*, "economists, myself included, have tended to underplay the disruptive effects of rapid change... many of us feel that we missed something important about the downsides of rapid globalization" (2021).

Figure 13: Trade Shock Increased "Deaths of Despair": Mortality per 100K among Adults Ages 20–39, 1990–2015

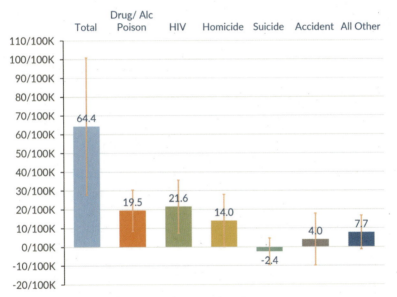

Source: Data from Autor, Dorn, and Hanson (2019)

The following figure from the Pew Research Center is potentially useful for understanding the political consequences of the China trade shock. The infographic (see Figure 14) shows that in 1994 only 64% of Republicans were to the right of the median Democrat and 70% of Democrats were to the left of the median Republican. While this skew may seem large, remember that if these groups had the same distribution of political preferences, still half of Democrats would be more liberal than the median Republican and half of Republicans would be more conservative than the median Democrat. Rolling the clock forward to 2017, however, we can see the coming apart of political consensus, with 95% of Republicans now more conservative than the median Democrat, and 97% of Democrats more liberal than the median Republican.

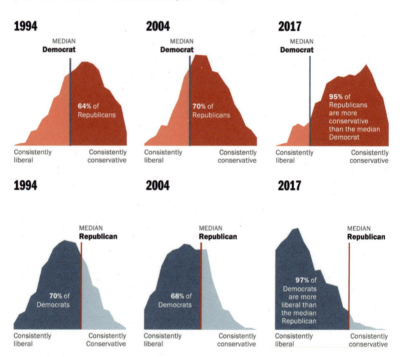

Figure 14: Political Polarization: Distribution of Republicans and Democrats on a 10-item Scale of Political Values, 1994–2017

Source: Pew Research Center (2017)

This increase in political polarization between 1994 and 2017 motivated me and my coauthors David Dorn, Gordon Hanson, and Kaveh Majlesi to ask the simple question: "has the trade shock contributed to this polarization?" Studying the outcome of Congressional elections, we do find evidence that the places more subjected to trade shocks became more likely to elect Republicans (see Figure 15), but not just any Republicans:

we observe a decline in moderate Republicans and moderate Democrats, and a rise in conservative Republicans (see Figure 16). Thus, the trade shock had the effect of hollowing out the middle of the political spectrum and shifting weight towards one tail in the most affected places. Evidence shows that the beneficiaries of this hollowing out were mostly, but not exclusively, on the right side of the political spectrum. Based on this evidence, we believe that the trade shock, through its disruptive political consequences, contributed to the rise of the highly conservative Tea Party movement in the House of Representatives. We stress that the trade shock was not the primary or exclusive cause of these outcomes but rather a catalyst.

Figure 15: Trade Shock Raised the Odds that Republicans Win House Seats, 2002–2016

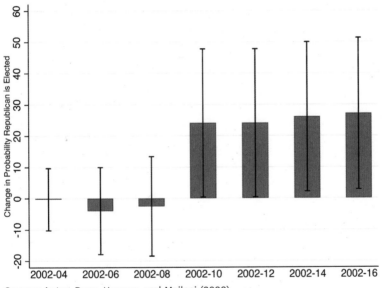

Source: Autor, Dorn, Hanson, and Majlesi (2020)

A natural question is whether these same shocks contributed to Donald Trump's unexpected presidential victory in 2016. The evidence suggests that the answer is yes. In a regression estimate, a 10% notional reduction of the trade shock would hypothetically have turned Michigan blue in the 2016 presidential election, and a 25% reduction would hypothetically have turned Wisconsin blue. A 50% reduction would, according to these estimates, have brought Pennsylvania to Democrats. This is, of course, a hypothetical exercise and should not be taken as definitive. The 2016 presidential election was an incredibly close one, meaning that many factors could have tipped the outcome in either direction. As it happened, some of the manufacturing-intensive local labor markets where these trade shocks were particularly pronounced were in swing states where election outcomes were relatively close to a toss-up. As such, the outcomes of these elections may have been swayed by the China trade shock. And of course, the political fallout continues to the present day.

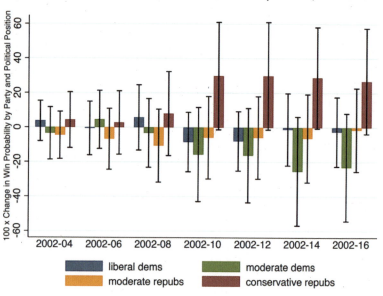

Figure 16: In House of Representatives, Trade Shock Wipes Out Moderate Republicans and Democrats, Ushers in Conservative Republicans, 2002–2016

Source: Autor, Dorn, Hanson, and Majlesi (2020)

Conclusion: five key takeaways

The United States would ultimately have shed its China-exposed jobs and sectors, even without the trade shock. High-wage industrialized countries generally are not competitive in labor-intensive industries, such as textiles or assembly of toys and dolls. However, the trade shock accelerated that process dramatically, and the rate of change is a crucial factor when considering the ability of people and places to effectively adjust to changed circumstances.

The "China shock" was also a catalyst of US polarization. But it was not the exclusive cause. We know this because similar political forces are at play in other liberal democracies that were not exposed to the same intensity of shock. One can see the rise of populist candidates, for example, in the Netherlands, Sweden, Germany, and France. Indeed, Germany's labor market was arguably a substantial net beneficiary of China's rise, but this has not insulated Germany from political polarization.

Something that has received insufficient attention is the degree to which the NAFTA trade policy of 1994 was a prequel to the China trade shock, both in its economic and political consequences. An in-press paper by Choi, Kuziemko, Washington, and Wright shows how NAFTA policies had both important employment effects and profound political consequences. By the time the Clinton administration was pushing NAFTA through Congress, blue-collar voters in the South were already hanging on to the Democratic Party by a thread, and that thread was trade protection and union protection. Cutting that thread severed that group of voters from the Democratic Party. Although those voters were neither politically nor ideologically aligned with the liberal values of the Democratic Party at that point, they were aligned with the party on worker protection. And so, arguably, the NAFTA policy provided momentum to this slow-moving but now extremely visible parting of ways between Democrats and blue-collar voters.

The China trade shock, as we knew it, is now over, however. China is in a different era economically, and the US and China are in different eras strategically. We are no longer fighting about who makes textiles and assembles dolls. Those were the easy days.

It is finally useful to ask what should we have foreseen about the consequences of the China trade shock, and what can only be understood in hindsight? The economic policy that helped to accelerate the trade shock – China being granted Normal Trade Relations (PNTR) status with the US in 2000 and gaining WTO membership in 2001 – was propelled by a belief in Washington that bringing China into the world trading system would encourage this vast, rapidly developing and increasingly powerful country to join the fold of democratic nations. This did not occur. If, hypothetically, China had not been admitted to the WTO and had not been granted PNTR, and yet were we facing similar geopolitical circumstances as we do today, many experts (likely myself included) would blame current US tensions with China on the US having barred China from fully entering the world trading system two decades earlier. The lesson, I think, is that the present poor state of US-China relations was not readily forecastable. Had we made different decisions two decades earlier, we might draw the wrong lessons from them today.

What economists and policymakers could certainly have better anticipated is the deep economic distress that China's entry into the world trading system would ultimately mean for manufacturing-intensive communities in the United States. Had policymakers applied such foresight, they could have enacted social insurance policies and public investment programs to insulate, compensate, and retrain workers, to buffer the transition for trade-affected communities, and broadly, to reduce economic dislocation while spurring new employment. Absent such policies, the ensuing economic scars were deeper and slower to heal. While we could not have fully anticipated the scale, shape, or political trajectory of the China trade shock, the disruptive impact of trade openings on workers employed in import-competing sectors has long been understood. That the US failed to foresee and ameliorate these impacts is a homegrown policy failure, not a Chinese import.

References

Autor, David. 2017. "Economic and Political Consequences of China's Rise for the United States: Lessons from the China Shock." *Institute for Fiscal Studies, The Royal Society, London.*

Autor, David. 2022. "The Enduring Consequences of the China Trade Shock: Myths and Measurement." *Nobel Symposium on Inequality.*

Autor, David, David Dorn and Gordon H. Hanson. 2013. "The China Syndrome: Local Labor Effects of Import Competition in the United States," *American Economic Review*, 103(6), pp. 2121–2168.

Autor, David, David Dorn and Gordon H. Hanson. 2016a. "The China Shock: Learning from Labor Market Adjustment to Large Changes in Trade," *Annual Review of Economics*, 8(2016), pp. 205–240.

Autor, David, David Dorn and Gordon H. Hanson. 2016b. Regional Economics, "Chapter 2: Globalization and the China Trade Shock," *Malcolm Wiener Center for Social Policy, Harvard Kennedy School.*

Autor, David, David Dorn and Gordon H. Hanson. 2019. "When Work Disappears: Manufacturing Decline and the Falling Marriage-Market Value of Men," *American Economic Review: Insights*, 1(2), pp. 161–178.

Autor, David, David Dorn and Gordon H. Hanson. 2021. "On the Persistence of the China Shock," Brookings Papers on Economic Activity, Fall 2021, pp. 381–447.

Autor, David, David Dorn, Gordon H. Hanson and Kaveh Majlesi. 2020. "Importing Political Polarization? The Electoral Consequences of Rising Trade Exposure," *American Economic Review*, 110(10), pp. 3139–3183.

Case, Anne and Angus Deaton. 2020. *Deaths of Despair and the Future of Capitalism*. Princeton University Press.

Choi, Jiwon, Ilyana Kuziemko, Ebonya L. Washington and Gavin Wright. 2021. "Local Economic and Political Effects of Trade Deals: Evidence from NAFTA," NBER Working Paper 29525, forthcoming *American Economic Review.*

Dorn, David and Peter Levell. 2021. "Trade and Inequality in Europe and the United States," *IFS Deaton Review of Inequalities*, November 16, 2021. https://doi.org/10.5167/uzh-215628

Grewal, David Singh. 2022. "A World-Historical Gamble: The Failure of Neoliberal Globalization," *American Affairs Journal*, VI(4), pp. 87–121.

Krugman, Paul. 1997. "What Should Trade Negotiators Negotiate About?," *Journal of Economic Literature*, 35(1), pp. 113–120.

Krugman, Paul. 2021. "Krugman Wonks Out: The China Shock and the Climate Shock," *New York Times*, April 23, 2021.

Krugman, Paul and Maurice Obstfeld. 2008. *International Economics: Theory and Policy*, 8th Edition. Pearson, College Division.

Pew Research Center. 2017. "The Partisan Divide on Political Values Grows Even Wider."

Rodrigue, Jean-Paul et al. 2020. The Geography of Transport Systems, Hofstra University, Department of Global Studies & Geography.

Van Dam, Andrew and Jessica Ma. 2016. "The Parts of America Most Vulnerable to China." *Wall Street Journal*. https://graphics.wsj.com/china-exposure/

Wilson, William Julius. 1996. *When Work Disappears: The World of the New Urban Poor*. Vintage Press.

III

Policy and Performance
in the Illiberal Turn:
Money and Growth

Populist Leadership and Economic Decline[1]

MORITZ SCHULARICK
Kiel Institute for the World Economy & Sciences Po

CHRISTOPH TREBESCH
Kiel Institute for the World Economy

MANUEL FUNKE
Kiel Institute for the World Economy

Introduction

Most work on populism has investigated the reasons why voters choose populist leaders and governments. In our new research (Funke et al., 2023), we study the economic and political costs of populism and find that it leads to slower economic growth, undermines democratic institutions, and can leave a country more vulnerable to future populist governments.

The rise of populism in the past two decades has motivated much work on the determinants of populist voting (see the review by Guriev and Papaioannou, 2020, or Guiso et al., 2017, and Rodrik, 2017). In contrast, we still have limited knowledge of the economic and political consequences of populism. How does the economy perform after populists come to power? Is populism a threat to liberal democracy or not?

---

1   This is an abridged, edited, and updated version of the article "Populist Leaders and the Economy" by Manuel Funke, Moritz Schularick, and Christoph Trebesch, published in the *American Economic Review* in December 2023. To parts of this text and the figures the following copyright notice may apply: Copyright American Economic Association; reproduced with permission.

These questions have not been sufficiently addressed. Moreover, most existing analyses focus on individual countries or data just from the past 20 or 30 years. What is missing is a bigger picture and a global, long-run perspective.

To address these questions, in a new paper (Funke et al., 2023) we built a comprehensive cross-country database on populism, identifying 51 populist presidents and prime ministers in the period 1900–2020. To code populist leaders, we rely on today's workhorse definition in political science, according to which populism is a political strategy that focuses on the conflict between "the people" and "the elites" (e.g., Mudde, 2004). Precisely, we define a leader as populist if he or she places the alleged struggle of the people ("us") against the elites ("them") at the center of their political campaign and governing style (for example, based on this definition, Putin, Reagan, or Obama cannot be classified as populists, but Bolsonaro, Berlusconi, or Trump clearly can).

For coding, we collected, digitized, and evaluated more than 20,000 pages of scientific literature on populism and identified 51 leaders who clearly fit the above definition of a populist politician. More specifically, we evaluated approximately 1,500 leaders (i.e., president, prime minister, or equivalent) in 60 countries starting in 1900 or the year in which the country achieved independence. We started in 1900 since there is little evidence of populists in government at the federal level prior to that date (in 1896 the populist William Jennings Bryan ran for president in the US but lost).

Using this sample, we conducted a historical analysis of the ups and downs of populist leadership worldwide over the past 120 years and gauged its political and economic fallout.

Populism has a long history and it is serial in nature

Figure 1 summarizes the historical evolution of populism, by plotting the proportion of independent countries in our sample of 60 countries governed by populists each year since 1900 (bold red line). The figure shows that populism at the country level has existed for more than 100 years, and that it has reached a historical high in the past decade.

The first populist president was Hipólito Yrigoyen, who came to power in the general election of Argentina in 1916. Since then, there have been two main populist peaks: during the Great Depression of the 1930s and in the 2010s. The 1980s was the low point for populists in power. However, after the fall of the Berlin Wall, from 1990 onward, populism returned with a vengeance. The year 2018 marked an all-time high, with 16 countries governed by leaders described by the political science literature as populists (more than 25% of the sample). This most recent increase can mainly be attributed to the emergence of a new populist right in Europe and beyond.

Figure 1: Populists in Power: Share of Countries in Sample

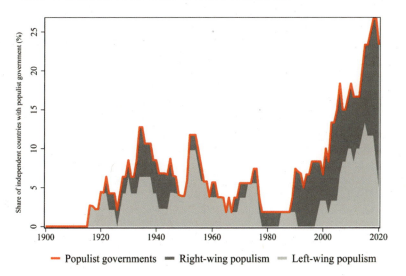

Source: Funke et al. (2023)

A particularly interesting insight from our long-run data is the reoccurrence of patterns of populism over time. Figure 2 shows the 27 countries (from our 60-country sample) that have a history of populist leadership (i.e., at least one populist government in power since 1900 or independence). For each country, the grey bars represent periods of populist leadership.

The key message from Figure 2 is that populism at the government level appears to be serial in nature, as it is observable in the same countries again and again. We identify long and repeating periods of populist rule, and establish that having been governed by a populist in the past is a strong predictor of populist rule in a country in recent years. Interestingly, half of the countries in Figure 2 with recurring periods of populist leadership saw switches from left-wing to right-wing populism or vice versa.

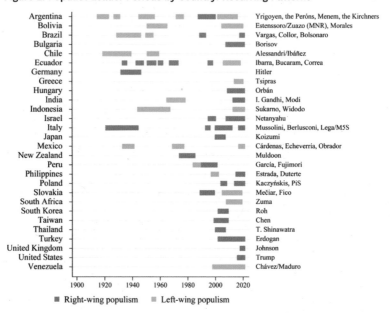

Figure 2: Populist Leader Periods by Country: Recurring Patterns

Source: Funke et al. (2023)

Populism has high economic costs

Figure 3 gives a hint of the economic consequences we can expect from the global surge of populist politics in recent years. Panel A shows four unconditionally averaged performance gaps in annualized real GDP growth after populists come to power, inspired by Blinder and Watson's (2016) measurement of a Democrat–Republican president performance gap in US postwar data. Countries underperformed by approximately one percentage point per year after a populist came to power, both compared to their country's typical long-run growth rate (white bars) and the (then-)current global growth rate (grey bars). This is true for the short term of five years and the long term of 15 years after a populist gains power.

The results in Panel A are unconditional on economic events surrounding the populist entering office or year-over-year dynamics, and they do not use a strict control group. All this is especially important since the identification of countries as having populist governments is likely not random with regards to the economy.

This is why we get more rigorous in Panel B. We apply the synthetic control method (SCM) proposed by Abadie et al. (2010) to construct a doppelganger for each case, using an algorithm to determine which combination of "donor economies" matches the growth trend of a country with the highest possible accuracy before the populist comes to power.

Comparing the evolution of this synthetic doppelganger with actual data for the populist economy quantifies the aggregate costs of the populist "treatment". We take averages of the path around populists entering office and compare them to the average estimated counterfactual path. Subtracting the synthetic control from the treated series results in the doppelganger gap that measures the average growth difference due to populism.

Panel B displays the results of this exercise. The blue line is the average difference (or gap) in GDP dynamics between treated (populist) and synthetic control (non-populist) groups, using a time horizon of 15 years before and after the entry into power (the red and black lines represent the left-wing and the right-wing populist dimension, respectively). We use simulation-based confidence intervals (CI; 90%) following Cattaneo et al. (2021, 2022).

The cumulative difference to the doppelganger economy is large, exceeding ten percentage points after 15 years. The GDP path starts to diverge visibly from the synthetic counterfactual soon after populists enter government, and the economy does not recover.

Figure 3: The Economic Costs of Populism: Average GDP Growth Gaps

Panel A: Unconditional annual loss (in percentage points, pp)

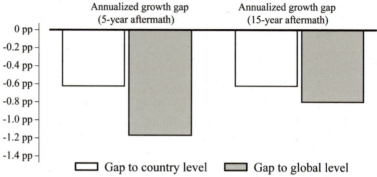

Panel B: Loss compared to synthetic control group (in %, relative to entry into office)

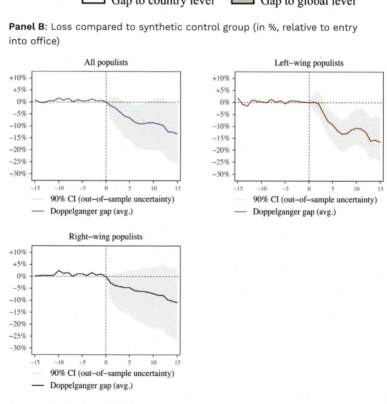

Source: Funke et al. (2023)

Importantly, all these results are robust not only when we cut the sample along the left-wing versus right-wing populist dimension, as can be seen, but also for several other dimensions: geographical region, historical era, length of the rule, and initial conditions, such as financial crises before/during the election year. We further conduct "country placebo" and "time placebo" tests that support our main results. The results also held when using SCMs that account for multiple treated units and staggered adoption (Abadie and L'Hour, 2021; Ben-Michael et al., 2021).

Figure 4: The Political Consequences of Populism: Institutional Decay

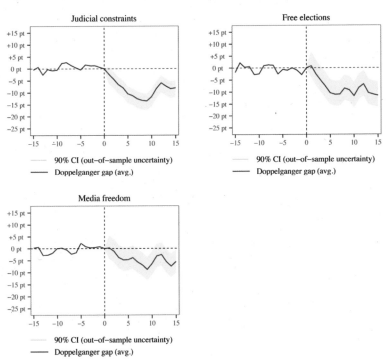

Source: Funke et al. (2023)

Figure 5: Core Government Policies Under Populists: Economic Disintegration, Debt, and Inflation

Panel A: Economic nationalism

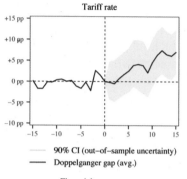

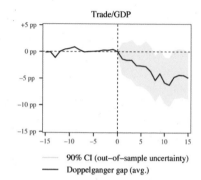

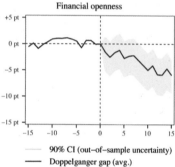

Panel B: Macroeconomic policies

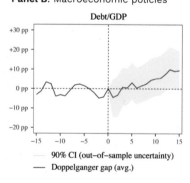

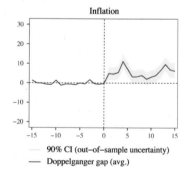

Source: Funke et al. (2023)

Populism is politically disruptive

Populism is also costly for democratic institutions. To provide one example, we study the evolution of executive constraints. Figure 4 shows SCM results for all populists in our sample (similar to the blue line in Panel B of Figure 3 on GDP), using indices of judicial constraints on executive, electoral, and media freedom from the Varieties of Democracy (V-Dem) database. Higher values indicate a higher degree of institutional strength. As can be seen, these checks and balances decline markedly after populists come to power, especially when compared to the non-populist counterfactual. These results are again robust to cutting the sample across left-wing and right-wing cases. The erosion of democratic norms may explain both the persistence and the negative economic outcomes of populism (e.g., Acemoglu et al., 2005, 2013, 2019; Guriev and Treisman, 2019).

Economic nationalism and unsustainable macroeconomic policies

Regarding the impact on growth, we also found confirming evidence for two other channels that are core fields of government policy and that also play a prominent role in the populism literature: economic nationalism, in particular via protectionist trade policies (e.g., Born et al., 2019), and the classic Sachs (1989) and Dornbusch and Edwards (1991) macro-populism studies on unsustainable macroeconomic policies, resulting in spiraling public debt and inflation. The results, again using the SCM, are reported in Figure 5.

Conclusion

When populists come to power, they can do lasting economic and political damage. Countries governed by populists witness a substantial decline in real GDP per capita, on average. Protectionist trade policies, unsustainable debt dynamics, and the erosion of democratic institutions stand out as commonalities of populists in power.

Looking ahead, a major risk is the serial nature of populism. The historical data we gathered suggest that populism is a persistent phenomenon, with countries like Argentina and Ecuador witnessing on-and-off populist leadership all the way back to 1916. The big question is whether advanced countries will share a similar fate going forward, witnessing "serial populism" for the next years and decades. Unfortunately, in the light of history, this is not an unlikely scenario.

References

Abadie, A., A. Diamond, and J. Hainmueller (2010), "Synthetic control methods for comparative case studies: Estimating the effect of California's tobacco control program", *Journal of the American Statistical Association* 105(490): 493–505.

Abadie, A. and J. L'Hour (2021), "A Penalized Synthetic Control Estimator for Disaggregated Data", *Journal of the American Statistical Association* 116(536): 1817–1834.

Acemoglu, D., G. Egorov, and K. Sonin (2013), "A Political Theory of Populism", *The Quarterly Journal of Economics* 128(2): 771–805.

Acemoglu, D., S. Johnson, and J. A. Robinson (2005), "Institutions as the Fundamental Cause of Long-Run Growth", in: Agion, P. and S. Durlauf (eds.), *Handbook of Economic Growth*, Vol 1A: 385–472, Elsevier.

Acemoglu, D., S. Naidu, P. Restrepo, and J. A. Robinson (2019), "Democracy Does Cause Growth", *Journal of Political Economy* 127(1): 47–100.

Ben-Michael, E., A. Feller, and J. Rothstein (2021), "Synthetic Controls with Staggered Adoption", NBER Working Paper No. 28886.

Blinder, A. S. and M. W. Watson (2016), "Presidents and the US Economy: An Econometric Exploration", *American Economic Review* 106(4): 1015–1045.

Born, B., G. J. Müller, M. Schularick, and P. Sedlacek (2019), "The Cost of Economic Nationalism: Evidence from the Brexit Experiment", *Economic Journal* 129(623): 2722–2744.

Cattaneo, M. D., Y. Feng, and R. Titiunik (2021), "Prediction Intervals for Synthetic Control Methods", *Journal of the American Statistical Association* 116(536): 1865–1880.

Cattaneo, M. D., Y. Feng, F. Palomba, and R. Titiunik (2022), "scpi: Uncertainty Quantification for Synthetic Control Estimator", Working Paper, February 2022.

Dornbusch, R. and S. Edwards (eds.) (1991), *The Macroeconomics of Populism in Latin America*, University of Chicago Press.

Funke, M., M. Schularick, and C. Trebesch (2023), "Populist Leaders and the Economy", *American Economic Review* 113(12): 3249–3288.

Guiso, L., H. Herrera, M. Morelli, and T. Sonno (2017), "The spread of populism in Western countries", VoxEU.org, 14 October 2017.

Guriev, S. and E. Papaioannou (2020), "The Political Economy of Populism", CEPR Discussion Paper No. 14433.

Guriev, S. and D. Treisman (2019), "Informational Autocrats", *Journal of Economic Perspectives* 33(4): 100–127.

Mudde, C. (2004), "The populist zeitgeist", *Government and Opposition* 39(4): 541–563.

Rodrik, D. (2017), "Economics of the populist backlash", VoxEU.org, 03 July 2017.

Sachs, J. D. (1989), "Social conflict and populist policies in Latin America", NBER Working Paper No. 2897.

The Politics and Limits of Monetary Policy Under Growing Authoritarianism: The Case of Turkey

AYCA ZAYIM
Mount Holyoke College

Turkey was the darling of the international financial community until a few years ago. It received praise for its thriving economy and steady progress toward liberal democracy from international financial institutions, investors, and observers. The World Bank's 2014 Turkey Country Snapshot (2014), for instance, argued that Turkey's "rapid economic and social progress" was an "inspiration to reformers," "hold[ing] many useful lessons for policy makers in other emerging markets" (p. 2). Turkey is no more. "Once a beacon of democratic consolidation in a volatile neighborhood" (Kirişci and Sloat, 2019), it is now a worrisome case of democratic backsliding. It suffers from triple-digit inflation, a collapsing currency, rapidly accumulating external debt, and declining living standards for the majority of its population. Dubbed a "mess" (Askew, 2022), it is seen as an economy that is "caught in a spiral of lira crises" (Strohecker, 2022) and "in pressing need of reform and repair" (*The Economist*, 2023b). But what went wrong? How did a seeming success story turn into a disaster?

Most blame President Erdogan's growing authoritarianism and his oft-called "bizarre" or "mad" economic policies (e.g., *The Economist*, 2022). Following a failed coup attempt in July 2016, President Erdogan and the AKP (*Adalet ve Kalkınma Partisi* – Justice and Development Party) government declared a prolonged state of emergency during which there was a forceful crackdown on the opposition. Thousands of civil society and media organizations, politicians, journalists, and human rights activists were targeted; some were imprisoned (Yılmaz, 2020). A constitutional referendum was held in the following year that ratified Turkey's move from a parliamentary system to a heavily centralized presidential system. The reforms entailed a drastic institutional reconfiguration of the state and gave new powers to the president with few checks and balances (Öniş and Kutlay, 2021). In June 2018, Erdogan was re-elected as the president under the new regime. Freedom House (2018) downgraded Turkey's status from "partly free" to "not free" that same year, pointing to deteriorating political rights and civil liberties.

The presidential system also brought unprecedented changes to macroeconomic management. Based on the president's newly acquired powers, such as the right to issue decrees, propose the national budget, and appoint high-level bureaucrats with little oversight, President Erdogan effectively established "de facto and de jure executive control" over the Turkish central bank, officially known as the Central Bank of the Republic of Turkey (CBRT) (Apaydin and Çoban, 2023, p. 1,060). This was no surprise. Right before the 2018 presidential election, Erdogan had denounced interest rates as "the mother and father of all evil" and assured his supporters that his re-election would mean a "victory in the fight against this curse of interest rates" (Kucukgocmen and Taner, 2018). Days later, he spoke with Bloomberg in London, unequivocally revealing his intentions to intervene in the central bank's decisions. He replied to the question of whether he would play a role in monetary policy as follows: "Yes! This may make some uncomfortable. But we have to do it... Of course, our central bank is independent, but the central bank can't take this independence and set aside the signals given by the president, who's the head of the executive. It will make its evaluations according to this, take its steps according to this" (Ant and Demokan, 2018). The financial community was in "shock and disbelief" (Strohecker, 2018) following Erdogan's message, and the *Financial Times* (2018a) reported that investors "were wondering whether there was any longer an argument for risking their money in his country's currency, stocks, and government bonds." It seemed that Erdogan had waged a war against the orthodoxy of central bank independence.

Although the regime shift has been significant in Turkey's authoritarian turn, scholars and observers point to a gradual process of democratic backsliding in Turkey at least since 2011, describing the two-decade rule by AKP as "authoritarian neoliberalism" (Adaman and Akbulut, 2021; Akça, 2014; Akçay, 2021; Tansel, 2018), "anti-democratic populism" (Rogenhofer and Panievsky, 2020), or "competitive authoritarianism" (Çalışkan, 2018; Castaldo, 2018; Esen and Gumuscu, 2016; Özbudun, 2015). During his tenure as Prime Minister and President between 2003 and 2018, Erdogan's relationship with the central bank and the financial community had already been far from harmonious. Erdogan's contentious pronouncements intensified especially after 2013, and occasionally other AKP members joined him. As an outspoken critic of the central bank, Erdogan would frequently express a preference for low interest rates, citing Islamic teachings which supposedly ban collecting interest. He was also a champion of his self-proclaimed "theory" that high inflation was the result of high interest rates – a view often ridiculed by academic economists (e.g., *The Economist*, 2022). During the 2013 Gezi protests, Erdogan accused domestic and foreign financial institutions of stirring political unrest and benefiting from the resultant high interest rates, calling them the "interest rate lobby" (Saglam, 2013). He later labeled anyone who criticized his economic views as the interest rate lobby and denounced their activities as "treason against the nation" (Reuters, 2015). In May 2014, Erdogan once again expressed his contempt for the central bank for pursuing tighter-than-desired monetary policy. "I told them several times," he said, "This is outrageous. Don't mess with people with a half-point cut" (Haberturk, 2014). In February 2015, he targeted central bank governor Basci, saying, "The central bank's interest rate policy is unsuited to the realities of the Turkish economy… You are conducting a struggle for independence against us, but are you dependent on some other places [people]?" (Coskun, 2015). The public scolding fueled widespread rumors that Basci and Deputy Prime Minister Babacan – a longtime friend and supporter of Basci – would resign. The news rattled investors. A few days later, Erdogan further asked the two men to "shape up" as they were supposedly on a "wrongful path" (NTV, 2015).

Governor Basci (2011–2016) and his successor Cetinkaya (2016–2019) strove hard to thwart the political pressure to deliver rock-bottom interest rates. During my research, I found that they did this by manipulating the central bank's unconventional monetary policy framework known as the "asymmetric interest rate corridor". This framework was initially designed to ward off hot money inflows during 2011 but was later revised to enhance the flexibility of monetary policy. In an effort to balance the competing pressures on the central bank, policymakers used the framework to deliver what was colloquially known as "stealth interest rate hikes."[1] Central bankers would keep the official policy rate low while effectively funding financial institutions at a higher interest rate. This imperfect strategy continued until May 2018 when a rapid depreciation of the Turkish lira fueled fears of a currency crisis. "After weeks of resisting action to arrest the sliding currency," the *Financial Times* (2018b) reported, Erdogan was "forced to submit to the power of the markets and allow the central bank to lift interest rates." The unconventional framework was also abandoned. Although markets "had won" this time (Ant, 2018), central bank governor Cetinkaya was sacked in July 2019 for "not listening." This is how Erdogan boasted about this decision a few months later: "Because we have changed the system, we also got the authority to remove the central bank [governor] from office... We removed the previous governor because he wasn't listening... We told him repeatedly in economy meetings that he should cut rates. We told him that the rate cut would help inflation fall. He didn't do what was necessary" (Sozcu, 2019). As a self-declared "enemy of interest rates" (Tol, 2021), Erdogan changed the central bank governor three more times between 2019 and 2022.

Generally speaking, Erdogan's monetary policy approach can be summarized as an uncompromising commitment to low interest rates – regardless of its costs. This was most clearly revealed during 2021 when nearly all central banks tightened monetary policy to fight soaring inflation. In fact, among a large sample of countries listed by the IMF, the Turkish central bank was the only central bank that eased monetary policy (Adrian and Natalucci, 2022). This had severe consequences. The real interest rates became negative; the lira depreciated by 44% in 2021 and by 30% in 2022

---

1   This information was gathered in interviews by the author.

against the US dollar, making Turkey the "worst performing emerging economy" (Reuters, 2023; *Financial Times*, 2022; Toksabay and Gumrukcu, 2021). Especially noteworthy is the fact that Putin congratulated the Russian central bank in December 2021 for preventing a "Turkish-style crisis," saying, "I know that the real sector is unhappy with the increase in rates, but without it, we could have a situation similar to that in Turkey…I do not interfere in the work of the central bank" (Arkhipov and Andrianova, 2021). The lira's depreciation contributed to already high inflation. According to highly contested official figures, the inflation rate reached 86% in October 2022 – the highest in 25 years. As shown in Figure 1, after 2018 there emerged a growing and dramatic divergence between the central bank's inflation target and the annual inflation rate.

Figure 1: Inflation Target and Annual Inflation Rate (2002–2022)

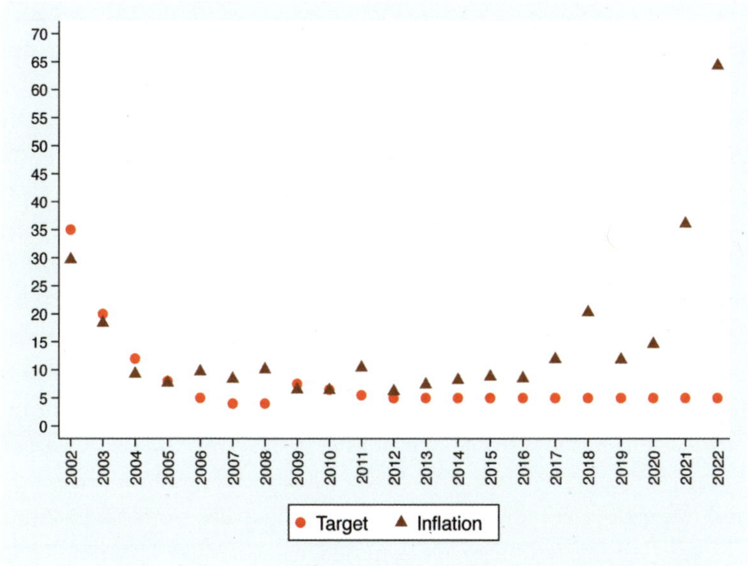

Source: Data from the Central Bank of the Republic of Turkey (CBRT, 2022b)

Admittedly, it has become increasingly common in recent years for populist and authoritarian leaders to criticize their central banks or to attempt to influence monetary policy decisions. Examples abound. For instance, Trump demanded that the Federal Reserve slash interest rates down to zero, calling central bankers "boneheads" and "pathetic," and claimed that he had "the right to fire" the chair of the Federal Reserve. The UK's shortest-serving prime minister Truss wanted to revisit the price stability mandate of the Bank of England. Orban undermined the Hungarian central bank's independence and appointed his self-claimed "right hand" as the bank's governor in 2013 to pursue financial nationalist policies. In India, Modi's appointee Das was pressured to cut rates prior to the 2019 elections and to transfer a record sum from the Reserve Bank to the government. In South Africa, a democratic nation with strong political and economic institutions, the ANC government has proposed expanding the central bank's mandate to include an explicit focus on employment and economic growth.

These examples might suggest that Erdogan is not alone. Yet, the Turkish case continues to remain a puzzle in some respects. Unlike the US, Turkey does not govern a reserve currency, and the country occupies a subordinate position in the global financial system. Additionally, unlike some other countries in the Global South (like India), Turkey has long been fully integrated into the global financial system and is heavily dependent on foreign capital inflows. A high degree of dependence on external financing is expected to discipline governments, pushing them to pursue economic policies that promote investor confidence (Block, 1977; Mahon, 1996; Mosley, 2003; Winters, 1996). In the case of central banking, this means the central bank should follow monetary orthodoxy and focus on price stability in line with the financial sector's preferences (Goodman, 1991; Maxfield, 1997; Posen, 1995). South Africa is a case in point. Not only did the recent government proposal face significant pushback from the central bank and the treasury due to South Africa's foreign financing needs, but it was also effectively "vetoed" by domestic and international financial investors. A local business newspaper aptly described the structural power exercised by the financial community in defeating the proposal: "Each time [changes to the central bank's mandate] is raised, markets react negatively, forcing [the] National Treasury and, more often than not, the presidency to come out and do damage control" (Businesstech, 2023). Another example is Hungary. Favorable global liquidity conditions in the post-crisis period and highly "tolerant" international investors allowed Orban to pursue financial nationalist policies (Johnson and Barnes, 2015). Once the global financial conditions changed, financial nationalism became less viable and there emerged a "rift" between Orban and the Hungarian central bank over high inflation (Szakacs and Than, 2023).

In light of these cases, what explains Turkey's unraveling commitment to low interest rates? And how long can it be sustained? Mainstream accounts point to Erdogan's religious beliefs and his long-held ideological convictions underlying his incessant defense of low interest rates. Notwithstanding the role played by these factors, I argue that low interest rates were critical to Erdogan's political success by supporting his macroeconomic populism within Turkey's financialized economy.

Following a severe financial crisis in 2001, Turkey implemented a series of neoliberal reforms under a comprehensive IMF-directed program. These reforms included the institutionalization of an independent central bank, banking sector regulation, the privatization of state banks and enterprises, and fiscal discipline, among others. When the first AKP government came to power in 2002, it had relatively narrow room to maneuver. Operating under tight budgetary constraints imposed by the IMF, it could not resort to excessive fiscal spending or push the central bank to monetize its debt. In this context, financialization became a crucial mechanism (Aklin and Kern, 2021) by which the AKP would maintain popular support. Financialization boosted economic growth and, along with financial inclusion, helped contain the adverse effects of neoliberal policies on lower- and middle-income groups. Accompanying financial inclusion, the AKP provided *selective* social protections that generated income gains for the urban poor and working class but did not forego fiscal discipline (Güven, 2016). During the first two terms of the AKP government, Turkey witnessed high and sustained economic growth rates with single-digit inflation alongside a dramatic reduction in government deficits. Thus, the government could have its cake and eat it too.

This strategy was helped by favorable external financial conditions that began around 2002 and continued until 2013 with a brief interruption with the collapse of Lehman Brothers (Akyuz, 2017). Throughout the 2000s, low interest rates in major economies, expanding global liquidity, and good economic prospects for emerging economies fueled capital inflows, generating rapid economic growth and currency appreciation in these economies (Akyuz, 2014). As Akyuz (2017, p. 85) describes, "a virtuous circle emerged whereby rapid growth attracted more capital into [emerging and developing economies] and this in turn added to growth by stimulating private spending in investment in property and consumption, thereby attracting even more capital." These dynamics became more pronounced after 2009. Due to "zero-bound" interest rates and quantitative easing in the Global North (Akyuz, 2017), there were ample low-cost foreign funding opportunities. Domestic interest rates could be kept relatively low and access to credit was fairly affordable and widespread among households and domestic firms in several economies.

Scholars describe the post-2001 Turkish economy as a "debt-led growth regime," "capital-inflows-dependent, finance-led growth model," "dependent financialization," or a "speculation-led economic growth model" (Akçay and Güngen, 2019; Bahçe et al., 2017; Orhangazi and Ozgur, 2015; Orhangazi and Yeldan, 2021). One characteristic of this growth regime has been external debt accumulation. Starting in the early 2000s, increased foreign capital inflows led to a significant appreciation of the Turkish lira. Coupled with relatively high domestic interest rates, both banks and non-financial corporations found it advantageous to borrow from abroad, mostly in foreign currency (FX). Consequently, external debt reached around 50% of GDP in 2014 (Orhangazi and Ozgur, 2015, p. 7). As shown in Figure 2, the share of government debt in external debt declined until the late 2010s, while that of financial and non-financial sectors dramatically increased. The external debt of non-financial corporations climbed from around $28 billion in 2004 to $86 billion in 2014, while that of financial institutions went from $20 billion to $127 billion (Çalışkan and Karimova, 2017, p. 1622). Furthermore, borrowing became more short-term. The share of short-term external debt reached 40% of the total external debt stock of financial and non-financial sectors in 2014 (ibid.).

A second pillar of the post-2001 growth regime has been domestic credit expansion. Capital inflows led to the appreciation of the lira and a decline in interest rates. While this has enhanced firms' and households' borrowing capacities, domestic banks took advantage of low-cost external financing opportunities and emerged as the financier of domestic credit growth. Total bank credit to non-financial corporations and households increased dramatically, as seen in Figure 3. Within household debt, credit card, housing, and personal loans accelerated, and the ratio of total consumer credit to GDP increased from 1.8% in 2002 to 18.7% in 2012 (Karacimen, 2014, p. 163).

Figure 2: Cumulative External Debt (USD billions)

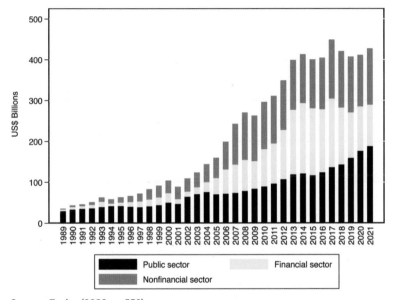

Source: Zayim (2022, p. 552)

This accompanied a construction boom, which was at the center of economic growth. After 2008, Turkey became one of the fastest-growing real estate markets in the world. "Construction-centered growth" was a deliberate accumulation strategy employed by the AKP (Orhangazi and Yeldan, 2021). Successive AKP governments effectively acted as a "developer and financier" in housing markets and engaged in a process of financialization whereby public urban land was commodified, mortgage markets were expanded, and low-income and poor households were integrated into the financial system through subsidized debt (Yeşilbağ, 2020). Through these processes, the construction sector served to cultivate loyalty and garner political support from urban lower- and middle-income groups. Additionally, the AKP governments used various construction projects to build a loyal business class through public procurement, construction permits, cheap credit, and tax reliefs (Esen and Gumuscu, 2018; Gürakar, 2016; Ocaklı, 2018). In particular, five pro-government construction companies – dubbed "the gang of five" by the main opposition leader – handsomely benefited from Turkey's new "land-based accumulation" (Yeşilbağ, 2022).

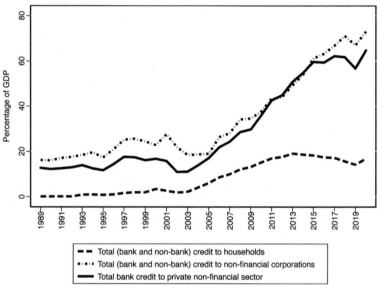

Figure 3: Domestic Credit Growth (1989–2020)[2]
Source: Zayim (2022, p. 553)

Although construction companies were at the forefront of pro-Erdogan domestic capital, the AKP's crony and clientelistic ties extended beyond the construction sector. The AKP promoted small and medium-sized enterprises and select big businesses on the rise with cheap credit and tax reliefs. In particular, state banks were used as a vehicle to distribute credit on very favorable terms (Apaydin and Çoban, 2023). In return for favorable

2   This covers the private non-financial sector, which includes households, non-financial corporations, and non-profit institutions serving households.

business contracts and deals, business groups supported the AKP governments with "their investments in pro-government media, in-kind donations to the party as well as to pro-AKP charities, and campaign contributions" (Esen and Gumuscu, 2018, p. 361). The AKP then distributed these donations to certain disadvantaged groups and used the selectively distributed social welfare goods, jobs, and charitable goods in exchange for political support (Buğra, 2020; Eder, 2010). Thus, a network of relationships "riddled with redistribution, favoritism, clientelism, and corruption" was built (Esen and Gumuscu, 2020, p. 1,080), extending to businesspeople (Buğra and Savaşkan, 2014; Esen and Gumuscu, 2018; Gürakar, 2016; Özcan and Gündüz, 2015) and the urban poor (Ark-Yıldırım, 2017; Yıldırım, 2020).

The favorable external financial conditions that underlay this clientelistic system came to a halt in 2013. When the US Federal Reserve announced its intention to roll back its quantitative easing program, in what became known as the tapering talk, the news altered investors' perceptions and led to a sharp decline in capital inflows to emerging economies (Rai and Suchanek, 2014). Although investors subsequently returned to these economies (to different degrees), capital inflows continued to decline during the Fed's tapering of bond purchases in 2014, and net inflows turned negative in the weeks before the Fed raised its policy rate in December 2015 (Akyuz, 2017). Capital outflows depressed stock and bond markets and put pressure on local currencies to depreciate. In particular, countries with sustained current account deficits were badly hit, such as Brazil, South Africa, and Turkey (ibid). There was a clear expectation within the financial community that central banks in these contexts would need to increase their policy rates. Inaction would tarnish central bank credibility, accelerating capital flight and currency depreciation and even triggering a crisis (Zayim, 2020).

The changing global liquidity conditions created a dilemma for the AKP and its leader Erdogan (Akçay, 2021; Altınörs and Akçay, 2022; Apaydin and Çoban, 2023). On the one hand, a tighter monetary policy was perceived as necessary by financial investors and constrained policymakers' choices. On the other hand, low interest rates helped sustain the AKP's clientelistic relationships and were therefore key to Erdogan's political survival. Monetary tightening would increase the cost of credit and limit its availability to households and domestic firms. This would be especially problematic for small and medium-sized enterprises with little access to international borrowing and for construction companies that thrive on cheap loans and high domestic demand. A slowdown in the economy would furthermore result in greater unemployment, disproportionately hurting low-income groups and the urban poor. Recent scholarship points to these contradictions to explain Erdogan's growing authoritarianism (Akçay, 2021; Altınörs and Akçay, 2022; Apaydin and Çoban, 2023). From this perspective, Erdogan's increasingly contentious relationship with the central bank since 2013 and his eventual takeover of monetary policy after 2018 could be read as a desperate effort to sustain this financialized growth regime and the clientelistic relationships it feeds in a changing global financial context.

How long can this effort be sustained given its disastrous consequences? Despite the rhetoric, the post-2018 period was highly contentious and marked by trial-and-error learning. Not only were there multiple governor appointments to the central bank, but the focus of monetary policy also oscillated between maintaining low interest rates and gaining investor confidence. After the sacking of central bank governor Cetinkaya in July 2019, the newly appointed governor Uysal rapidly lowered the policy rate from 24% to 8.25% in accordance with President Erdogan's demands. This was the highest cumulative rate cut in the world in 2019 (Bloomberg HT, 2020). To combat the depreciation pressures on the lira, Uysal and Albayrak – Erdogan's son-in-law and then Minister of Treasury and Finance – covertly sold an estimated $128 billion from the central bank reserves. This scandal would later cause a public uproar and become a key part of the political campaign against Erdogan in the 2023 elections. As Bloomberg (Ghosh, 2021) reported, "Turks and foreign investors alike want[ed] to know where $128 billion went." Despite tightening monetary policy and increasing the policy rate in September 2020, Uysal could not curb the lira's collapse. Due to his purported policy failures, Uysal was removed from office in November 2020 (*Financial Times*, 2020). Albayrak resigned one day later.

Agbal, a former finance minister, succeeded Uysal. In as little as two months, Agbal hiked the policy rate from 10.25% to 17% and communicated his strong intentions to fight inflation. In an interview with Reuters in

February 2021, for instance, he said: "It is obvious that a strong monetary tightening must be implemented in order... to restore the disinflation process as soon as possible, and that this will continue for a long time" (Coskun and Devranoglu, 2021). His actions during his four-month-long tenure were perceived by financial investors as a gradual move toward monetary policy orthodoxy and rebuilding the central bank's credibility. The financial community praised Agbal's focus on price stability and viewed his appointment as a signal that "Erdogan was ready to cede a degree of autonomy to the bank" (*Financial Times*, 2021a). In March 2021, Agbal further hiked the policy rate from 17% to 19%, exceeding the "market expectations". However, Agbal was fired without an explanation two days later. The *Financial Times* (2021b) reported that the decision "shocked" investors, fueling "a feeling of exasperation". A massive capital flight ensued and the lira collapsed by 14% against the US dollar following the announcement (*Financial Times*, 2021c). Subsequently, Kavcioglu took office, known for sharing Erdogan's unconventional views about interest rates and inflation. Kavcioglu's arrival at the bank "was met with a sharp market sell-off" (Reuters, 2021). While monetary policy during his nearly two-year term reflected Erdogan's commitment to low interest rates, foreign and (where possible) domestic investors left, the lira depreciated further, and inflation rose.

Erdogan and his team of macroeconomic policymakers were cognizant of the ways in which capital mobility constrained their room to maneuver. Faced with capital flight several times since 2018, they had been forced to hike interest rates and resort to orthodox monetary policy. They learned from this experience. Instead of responding to capital flight, they sought to prevent it in the first place. Starting in 2018, the AKP government gradually introduced what one interviewee described as "backdoor capital controls".[3] First, several amendments were made to the decree protecting the value of the Turkish currency, placing restrictions on foreign currency transactions by domestic residents and export firms. Then, more specific measures targeting domestic banks and corporations were taken, such as making it more difficult to bet against the lira, limiting the availability of

---

3   This information was gathered in an interview by the author.

bank loans to companies holding significant foreign-denominated assets, pushing domestic banks to buy government bonds, despite much lower yields, if their ratio of local currency-denominated assets to total assets was less than 50%, and requiring companies to sell their FX assets to access cheap lira-denominated bank loans (BDDK, 2022; CBRT, 2022a). These regulations aimed to contain the depreciation of the lira and to stabilize the exchange rate, but, more importantly, by weakening the veto power of domestic investors, they made the pursuit of low interest rates possible. In addition to capital regulations, policymakers secured external finance from sources outside of the Western-led international financial institutions. The central bank concluded currency swap agreements with China, Qatar, South Korea, and the United Arab Emirates, amounting to $27 billion in early 2022 (Sonmez, 2022). Russia wired billions to Turkey to finance the construction of a nuclear plant as a subsidiary of Rosatom (Kozok, 2022). Prior to the 2023 elections, Russia's energy company Gazprom also allowed Turkey to delay payments for its natural gas imports (Devranoglu and Coskun, 2023). Lastly, Turkey has received some capital inflows that are "unaccounted" for: in the first eight months of 2022, the "errors and omissions" in the balance of payments hit a surplus of $28 billion (Pitel and Samson, 2022). The source of these inflows is of much debate.

This brings forth an interesting paradox. Championed under the banner of "South-South cooperation", external financial support from the Global South has often been argued for to help developing countries escape IMF conditionality and pursue heterodox, developmental policies. However, these alternative sources of funding could also help prolong the rule of authoritarian leaders such as Erdogan. They expand these leaders' room to maneuver by easing funding constraints while skirting the IMF's well-known involvement in inspecting/preparing government budgets (which necessarily increases government accountability and transparency). Although the IMF conditionalities are infamous for imposing austerity, stripping developing countries of their autonomy, and tilting the income distribution in favor of high-income groups, bilateral financial agreements like swaps are unlikely to come as a free lunch. Moreover, the conditionalities attached to them remain opaque, thus deepening the democracy deficit. While this paints a bleak picture, Turkey's recent elections in

May 2023 tentatively suggest the limits of relying on bilateral agreements. Following another re-election victory, Erdogan appointed a new central bank governor and finance minister in June 2023, both of whom are known to support monetary orthodoxy. At her first monetary policy committee meeting, Erkan, the new Turkish central bank governor, raised the policy rate from 8.5% to 15% as the first step toward monetary tightening (CBRT, 2023). Many interpreted this shift as a U-turn given Turkey's ever-growing external financing needs and as an effort on the part of Erdogan to attract Western financial investors (*The Economist*, 2023a). While it is too soon to draw conclusions, it is possible that Turkey's dependence on foreign capital might eventually discipline Erdogan or perhaps even win him over.

References

Adaman, F. and Akbulut, B. (2021). Erdoğan's three-pillared neoliberalism: Authoritarianism, populism and developmentalism. *Geoforum*, 124, 279–289. https://doi.org/10.1016/j.geoforum.2019.12.013

Adrian, T. and Natalucci, F. (2022). Central Banks Hike Interest Rates in Sync to Tame Inflation Pressures. IMF Blog, 10 August 2022. https://www.imf.org/en/Blogs/Articles/2022/08/10/central-banks-hike-interest-rates-in-sync-to-tame-inflation-pressures

Akça, I. (2014). Hegemonic Projects in Post-1980 Turkey and the Changing Forms of Authoritarianism, in I. Akça, A. Bekmen and B. A. Özden (eds.), *Turkey Reframed: Constituting Neoliberal Hegemony* (pp. 13–46). London: Pluto Press.

Akçay, U. (2021). Authoritarian Consolidation Dynamics in Turkey. *Contemporary Politics*, 27(1), 79–104. https://doi.org/10.1080/13569775.2020.1845920

Akçay, U. and Güngen, A. R. (2019). The Making of Turkey's 2018–2019 Economic Crisis. *Institute for International Political Economy Berlin Working Paper*, 120/2019. https://www.ipe-berlin.org/fileadmin/institut-ipe/Dokumente/Working_Papers/ipe_working_paper_120.pdf

Aklin, M. and Kern, A. (2021). The Side Effects of Central Bank Independence. *American Journal of Political Science*, 65(4), 971–987. https://doi.org/10.1111/ajps.12580

Akyuz, Y. (2014). Internationalization of Finance and Changing Vulnerabilities in Emerging and Developing Economies *UNCTAD Discussion Papers*, No. 217.

Akyuz, Y. (2017). *Playing with Fire: Deepened Financial Integration and Changing Vulnerabilities of the Global South*. Oxford: Oxford University Press.

Altınörs, G. and Akçay, Ü. (2022). Authoritarian Neoliberalism, Crisis, and Consolidation: The Political Economy of Regime Change in Turkey. *Globalizations*, 19(7), 1029–1053. https://doi.org/10.1080/14747731.2021.2025290

Ant, O. (2018). How Markets Won: Erdogan Concedes a Hated Rate Hike to Save Lira. *Bloomberg*, 24 May 2018. https://www.bloomberg.com/news/articles/2018-05-24/how-markets-won-erdogan-concedes-a-hated-rate-hike-to-save-lira?sref=am1wYMj6

Ant, O. and Demokan, S. (2018). Transcript: Turkey's President on Monetary Policy, Politics. *Bloomberg*, 15 May 2018. https://www.bloomberg.com/news/articles/2018-05-15/transcript-turkey-s-president-on-monetary-policy-politics?in_source=embedded-checkout-banner&leadSource=uverify%20wall

Apaydin, F. and Çoban, M. K. (2023). The Political Consequences of Dependent Financialization: Capital Flows, Crisis and the Authoritarian Turn in Turkey. *Review of International Political Economy*, 30(3), 1046–1072. https://doi.org/10.1080/09692290.2022.2083658

Ark-Yıldırım, C. (2017). Political Parties and Grassroots Clientelist Strategies in Urban Turkey: One Neighbourhood at a Time. *South European Society and Politics*, 22(4), 473–490. https://doi.org/10.1080/13608746.2017.1406431

Arkhipov, I. and Andrianova, A. (2021). Putin Hails Central Bank for Averting Turkish-Style Crisis. *Bloomberg*, 23 December 2021. https://www.bloomberg.com/news/articles/2021-12-23/putin-praises-bank-of-russia-for-averting-turkish-style-crisis#xj4y7vzkg

Askew, J. (2022). Soaring Inflation and a Collapsing Currency: Why is Turkey's Economy in Such a Mess? *Euronews*, 9 November 2022. https://www.euronews.com/2022/11/09/everything-is-overheating-why-is-turkeys-economy-in-such-a-mess

Bahçe, S. et al. (2017). Financialisation and the Financial and Economic Crises: The Case of Turkey, in E. Hein, D. Detzer, and N. Dodig (eds.), *Financialisation and the Financial and Economic Crises* (pp. 275–298). London: Edward Elgar.

BDDK. (2022). Banking Regulation and Supervision Agency Decision No. 10250 (Bankacılık Düzenleme ve Denetleme Kurulu Kararı No. 10250). https://www.bddk.org.tr/Mevzuat/DokumanGetir/1127

Block, F. (1977). The Ruling Class Does Not Rule: Notes on the Marxist Theory of the State. *Socialist Revolution*, 7(7), 6–28.

BloombergHT. (2020). CBRT Governor Uysal Removed, New Governor is Ağbal (TCMB Başkanı Uysal görevden alındı, yeni başkan Ağbal). 7 November 2020. https://www.bloomberght.com/tcmb-baskani-uysal-gorevden-alindi-yeni-baskan-agbal-2268125

Buğra, A. (2020). Politics of Social Policy in a Late Industrializing Country: The Case of Turkey. *Development and Change*, 51(2), 442–462. https://doi.org/10.1111/dech.12566

Buğra, A. and Savaşkan, O. (2014). *New Capitalism in Turkey: The Relationship between Politics, Religion and Business*. Cheltenham: Edward Elgar.

Businesstech. (2023). Warning Over Repeated Attacks on South Africa's Reserve Bank. 13 Feb 2023. https://businesstech.co.za/news/finance/664457/warning-over-repeated-attacks-on-south-africas-reserve-bank/

Çalışkan, A. and Karimova, A. (2017). Global Liquidity, Current Account Deficit, and Exchange Rate Balance Sheet Effects in Turkey. *Emerging Markets Finance and Trade*, 53(7), 1619–1640. https://doi.org/10.1080/1540496X.2016.1216837

Çalışkan, K. (2018). Toward a New Political Regime in Turkey: From Competitive Toward Full Authoritarianism. *New Perspectives on Turkey*, 58, 5–33. https://doi.org/10.1017/npt.2018.10

Castaldo, A. (2018). Populism and Competitive Authoritarianism in Turkey. *Southeast European and Black Sea Studies*, 18(4), 467–487. https://doi.org/10.1080/14683857.2018.1550948

CBRT. (2022a). Monetary Policy and Liraization Strategy for 2023. https://www.tcmb.gov.tr/wps/wcm/connect/1c1885ca-b730-452a-86d3-c22b33dc0eac/2023%2BPara%2BPolitikası%2Bve%2BLiralaşma%2BStratejisi_123022_0945_ENG.pdf?MOD=AJPERES

CBRT. (2022b). *Statistical Data (Electronic Data Delivery System)*. https://www.tcmb.gov.tr/wps/wcm/connect/en/tcmb+en/main+page+site+area/data

CBRT. (2023). Press Release: Monetary Policy Decision, 22 June 2023. https://www.tcmb.gov.tr/wps/wcm/connect/en/tcmb+en/main+menu/announcements/press+releases/2023/ano2023-22

Coskun, O. (2015). Turkey's Erdogan Questions Whether Central Bank Under External Influence. *Reuters*, 25 February 2015. https://www.reuters.com/article/turkey-cenbank-erdogan/update-2-turkeys-erdogan-questions-whether-central-bank-under-external-influence-idUSL5N0VZ44P20150225

Coskun, O. and Devranoglu, N. (2021). Back-to-basics: Agbal Hopes This Time is Different at Turkey's Central Bank. *Reuters*, 18 February 2021. https://www.reuters.com/article/us-turkey-cenbank-agbal-newsmaker-idUSKBN2AI0MT

Devranoglu, N. and Coskun, O. (2023). Exclusive: Turkey Defers $600 Million Russian Energy Payment Under Deal-sources. *Reuters*, 10 May 2023. https://www.reuters.com/business/energy/turkey-defers-600-mln-russian-energy-payment-sources-2023-05-10/

The Economist. (2022). Is Recep Tayyip Erdogan's Monetary Policy as Mad as it Seems? 27 January 2022. https://www.economist.com/the-economist-explains/2022/01/27/is-recep-tayyip-erdogans-monetary-policy-as-mad-as-it-seems

The Economist. (2023a). Turkey's President Erdogan Shifts Towards Sane Economics. 4 June 2023. https://www.economist.com/europe/2023/06/04/turkeys-president-erdogan-shifts-towards-sane-economics

The Economist. (2023b). The Turkish Economy is in Pressing Need of Reform and Repair. 16 January 2023. https://www.economist.com/special-report/2023/01/16/the-turkish-economy-is-in-pressing-need-of-reform-and-repair

Eder, M. (2010). Retreating State? Political Economy of Welfare Regime Change in Turkey. *Middle East Law and Governance*, 2(2), 152–184. https://doi.org/10.1163/187633710X500739

Esen, B. and Gumuscu, S. (2016). Rising competitive authoritarianism in Turkey. *Third World Quarterly*, 37(9), 1581–1606. https://doi.org/10.1080/01436597.2015.1135732

Esen, B. and Gumuscu, S. (2018). Building a Competitive Authoritarian Regime: State–Business Relations in the AKP's Turkey. *Journal of Balkan and Near Eastern Studies*, 20(4), 349–372. https://doi.org/10.1080/19448953.2018.1385924

Esen, B. and Gumuscu, S. (2020). Why Did Turkish Democracy Collapse? A Political Economy Account of AKP's Authoritarianism. *Party Politics*, 27(6), 1075–1091. https://doi.org/10.1177/1354068820923722

Financial Times. (2018a). Investors Lose their Appetite for Turkey. 15 May 2018. https://www.ft.com/content/e41a56d6-5855-11e8-bdb7-f6677d2e1ce8

Financial Times. (2018b). Recep Tayyip Erdogan: Turkey's Strongman Grapples with the Markets. 25 May 2018. https://www.ft.com/content/0e6898bc-5ffe-11e8-ad91-e01af256df68

Financial Times. (2020). Erdogan Ousts Head of Turkish Central Bank After Lira Plunge. 6 November 2020. https://www.ft.com/content/4e65286e-a33b-49b2-a5c4-b21b5cfa01fb

Financial Times. (2021a). Erdogan Reverts to Type with Bank Governor's Sacking. 21 May 2021. https://www.ft.com/content/3c09ab00-db5c-4324-bd3b-3986e5360e50

Financial Times. (2021b). Investors Left Shocked After Erdogan Upends Turkey's Markets. 26 March 2021. https://www.ft.com/content/fb5f31e8-9189-494f-af39-466606fd00c1

Financial Times. (2021c). Turkey's Lira Tumbles After Erdogan Sacks Central Bank Chief. 22 March 2021. https://www.ft.com/content/6be3efd1-a8e9-47a8-abac-966db2d3cf93

Financial Times. (2022). Turkish Lira Steadies After Tumbling 44% in Tumultuous 2021. 27 January 2022. https://www.ft.com/content/ed5918a8-d699-417b-a0f8-4e947fee3dc7

Freedom House. (2018). Freedom in the World 2018: Turkey. https://freedomhouse.org/country/turkey/freedom-world/2018

Ghosh, B. (2021). Question Over Forex Reserves Rattles Turkey's Erdogan. *Bloomberg*, 22 April 2021. https://www.bloomberg.com/opinion/articles/2021-04-22/question-over-128-billion-in-foreign-exchange-reserves-rattles-turkey-s-erdogan?embedded-checkout=true

Goodman, J. B. (1991). The Politics of Central Bank Independence. *Comparative Politics*, 23(3), 329–349. https://doi.org/10.2307/422090

Gürakar, E. Ç. (2016). *Politics of Favoritism in Public Procurement in Turkey: Reconfigurations of Dependency Networks in the AKP Era*. New York: Palgrave MacMillan.

Güven, A. B. (2016). Rethinking Development Space in Emerging Countries: Turkey's Conservative Countermovement. *Development and Change*, 47(5), 995–1024. https://doi.org/10.1111/dech.12254

Haberturk. (2014). We'll Do Whatever is Necessary When His Time is Up ('Vakti dolar biz de gereğini yaparız'). 28 May 2014. https://www.haberturk.com/ekonomi/para/haber/952347-vakti-dolar-biz-de-geregini-yapariz

Johnson, J. and Barnes, A. (2015). Financial Nationalism and its International Enablers: The Hungarian Experience. *Review of International Political Economy*, 22(3), 535–569. http://www.jstor.org/stable/2467330

Karacimen, E. (2014). Financialization in Turkey: The Case of Consumer Debt. *Journal of Balkan and Near Eastern Studies*, 16(2), 161–180. https://doi.org/10.1080/19448953.2014.910393

Kirişci, K. and Sloat, A. (2019). The Rise and Fall of Liberal Democracy in Turkey: Implications for the West. *Democracy & Disorder*, Policy Brief, Brookings Institution. https://www.brookings.edu/wp-content/uploads/2019/02/FP_20190226_turkey_kirisci_sloat.pdf

Kozok, F. (2022). Russia Is Wiring Dollars to Turkey for $20 Billion Nuclear Plant. *Bloomberg*, 29 July 2022. https://www.bloomberg.com/news/articles/2022-07-29/russia-is-wiring-dollars-to-turkey-for-20-billion-nuclear-plant

Kucukgocmen, A. and Taner, B. S. (2018). Turkey's Erdogan Calls Interest Rates "Mother of All Evil"; Lira Slides. *Reuters*. https://www.reuters.com/article/us-turkey-currency/turkeys-erdogan-calls-interest-rates-mother-of-all-evil-lira-slides-idUSKBN1IC1NV

Mahon, J. E. (1996). *Mobile Capital and Latin American Development*. University Park: Pennsylvania State University Press.

Maxfield, S. (1997). *Gatekeepers of Growth the International Political Economy of Central Banking in Developing Countries*. Princeton: Princeton University Press.

Mosley, L. (2003). *Global Capital and National Governments*. Cambridge: Cambridge University Press.

NTV. (2015). Erdogan Warns Babacan, Says He will Talk to Erdem Basci ("Erdem Başçı'yla konuşacağız" diyen Erdoğan'dan Babacan'a uyarı!). https://www.ntv.com.tr/turkiye/erdem-basciyi-cagirip-konusacagiz,nenaninaNk6HpsTZqq4v4w#

Ocaklı, F. (2018). Reconfiguring State-Business Relations in Turkey: Housing and Hydroelectric Energy Sectors in Comparative Perspective. *Journal of Balkan and Near Eastern Studies*, 20(4), 373–387. https://doi.org/10.1080/19448953.2018.1385926

Öniş, Z. and Kutlay, M. (2021). The Anatomy of Turkey's New Heterodox Crisis: The Interplay of Domestic Politics and Global Dynamics. *Turkish Studies*, 22(4), 499–529. https://doi.org/10.1080/14683849.2020.1833723

Orhangazi, O. and Ozgur, G. (2015). Capital Flows, Finance-led Growth and Fragility in the Age of Global Liquidity and Quantitative Easing: The Case of Turkey. *PERI Working Paper Series*, Number 397. https://peri.umass.edu/publication/item/679-capital-flows-finance-led-growth-and-fragility-in-the-age-of-global-liquidity-and-quantitative-easing-the-case-of-turkey

Orhangazi, O. and Yeldan, E. (2021). The Re-making of the Turkish Crisis. *Development and Change*, 52(3), 460–503. https://doi.org/10.1111/dech.12644

Özbudun, E. (2015). Turkey's Judiciary and the Drift Toward Competitive Authoritarianism. *The International Spectator*, 50(2), 42–55. https://doi.org/10.1080/03932729.2015.1020651

Özcan, G. B. and Gündüz, U. (2015). Political Connectedness and Business Performance: Evidence from Turkish Industry Rankings. *Business and Politics*, 17(1), 41–73. https://doi.org/10.1515/bap-2013-0037

Pitel, L. and Samson, A. (2022). Turkish Finance Minister Defends Economic Links with Russia. *Financial Times*, 24 October 2022. https://www.ft.com/content/d1b33e56-2835-4d04-8387-ba1d8dc55646

Posen, A. (1995). Declarations Are Not Enough: Financial Sector Sources of Central Bank Independence. *NBER Macroeconomics Annual*, 10, 253–274.

Rai, V. and Suchanek, L. (2014). The Effect of the Federal Reserve's Tapering Announcements on Emerging Markets. *Bank of Canada Staff Working Paper*, 2014-50. https://www.bankofcanada.ca/wp-content/uploads/2014/11/wp2014-50.pdf

Reuters. (2015). Turkey's Erdogan Says High Interest Rate 'Lobby' Guilty of Treason. 28 February 2015. https://www.reuters.com/article/us-turkey-economy-erdogan/turkeys-erdogan-says-high-interest-rate-lobby-guilty-of-treason-idUSKBN0LW0Y520150228

Reuters. (2021). Revolving Door: Personnel Changes at Turkey's Central Bank. 14 October 2021. https://www.reuters.com/world/middle-east/revolving-door-personnel-changes-turkeys-central-bank-2021-10-14/

Reuters. (2023). Turkish Lira Falls to Record Low Near 19 to the Dollar. 9 March 2023. https://www.reuters.com/markets/currencies/turkish-lira-falls-record-low-near-19-dollar-2023-03-09/

Rogenhofer, J. M. and Panievsky, A. (2020). Antidemocratic Populism in Power: Comparing Erdoğan's Turkey with Modi's India and Netanyahu's Israel. *Democratization*, 27(8), 1394–1412. https://doi.org/10.1080/13510347.2020.1795135

Saglam, E. (2013). Erdogan Flips on Turkey's 'Interest Lobby'. *AL-Monitor*, 17 July 2013. https://www.al-monitor.com/originals/2013/07/erdogan-raises-interest-rates-gezi-park-protests.html

Sonmez, M. (2022). Turkey's Central Bank Continues Window Dressing with Currency Swaps. *AL-Monitor*, 26 January 2022. https://www.al-monitor.com/originals/2022/01/turkeys-central-bank-continues-window-dressing-currency-swaps

Sozcu. (2019). President Spoke Openly: The Governor Was Not Listening (Cumhurbaşkanı ilk kez bu kadar açık konuştu: Merkez Bankası Başkanı laf dinlemiyordu). 5 November 2019. https://www.sozcu.com.tr/2019/ekonomi/cumhurbaskani-ilk-kez-bu-kadar-acik-konustu-merkez-bankasi-baskani-laf-dinlemiyordu-5432100/

Strohecker, K. (2018). 'Disbelief': Investors in Turkey Stunned by Erdogan's Fight with Markets. *Reuters*, 15 May 2018. https://www.reuters.com/article/us-turkey-markets-investors/disbelief-investors-in-turkey-stunned-by-erdogans-fight-with-markets-idUSKCN1IG2Y1

Strohecker, K. (2022). Turkey Caught in a Spiral of Lira Crises. *Reuters*, 10 June 2022. https://www.reuters.com/markets/europe/turkey-caught-spiral-lira-crises-2022-06-10/

Szakacs, G. and Than, K. (2023). Hungary's Orban Hits Back at Central Bank in Growing Rift over High Inflation. *Reuters*, 9 March 2023. https://www.reuters.com/markets/europe/hungarys-orban-says-central-bank-money-supply-cuts-are-too-drastic-2023-03-09/

Tansel, C. B. (2018). Authoritarian Neoliberalism and Democratic Backsliding in Turkey: Beyond the Narratives of Progress. *South European Society and Politics*, 23(2), 197–217. https://doi.org/10.1080/13608746.2018.1479945

Toksabay, E. and Gumrukcu, T. (2021). Turkey's Lira Logs Worst Year in Two Decades Under Erdogan. *Reuters*, 31 December 2021. https://www.reuters.com/markets/europe/turkeys-lira-weakens-fifth-day-monetary-policy-worries-2021-12-31/

Tol, G. (2021). Why is Turkey's President Cutting Interest Rates, Spurring Inflation, and Lowering the Value of the Lira? *Diwan*. https://carnegie-mec.org/diwan/85896

Winters, J. A. (1996). *Power in Motion Capital Mobility and the Indonesian State*. Ithaca: Cornell University Press.

World Bank. (2014). *World Bank Group – Turkey Partnership: Country Program Snapshot* (April 2014). Washington, DC: World Bank.

Yeşilbağ, M. (2020). The State-Orchestrated Financialization of Housing in Turkey. *Housing Policy Debate*, 30(4), 533–558. https://doi.org/10.1080/10511482.2019.1670715

Yeşilbağ, M. (2022). Statecraft on cement: The politics of land-based accumulation in Erdoğan's Turkey. *Urban Studies*, 59(13), 2679–2694. https://doi.org/10.1177/00420980211044044

Yıldırım, K. (2020). Clientelism and Dominant Incumbent Parties: Party Competition in an Urban Turkish Neighbourhood. *Democratization*, 27(1), 81–99. https://doi.org/10.1080/13510347.2019.1658744

Yılmaz, Z. (2020). Erdoğan's Presidential Regime and Strategic Legalism: Turkish Democracy in the Twilight Zone. *Southeast European and Black Sea Studies*, 20(2), 265–287.

Zayim, A. (2020). Inside the Black Box: Credibility and the Situational Power of Central Banks. *Socio-Economic Review*, 20(2), 759–789. https://doi.org/10.1093/ser/mwaa011

Zayim, A. (2022). Financialized Growth and the Structural Power of Finance: Turkey's Debt-Led Growth Regime and Policy Response after the Crisis. *Politics & Society*, 50(4), 543–570. https://doi.org/10.1177/00323292221125566

Illiberalism on Europe's Periphery: A Critical Macrofinance Tale

DANIELA GABOR
University of the West of England, Bristol

Introduction

Hungary has been Europe's poster child for illiberal democracy for the last decade. But throughout 2022–2023 it faced sustained inflationary pressures that threatened the Orbán regime. This led to unions mobilizing to protest real wage cuts, queues at petrol pumps, ineffective price controls, local capitalists angry at tax increases, and, perhaps most surprising, a public conflict between Viktor Orbán and György Matolcsy, the governor of the Hungarian Central Bank (the MNB), over anti-inflationary measures. Once Orbán's close political ally, Matolcsy denounced the government's price controls as failed socialism. In turn, Orbán first questioned 'overly contractionary' monetary policy, as Erdogan did in Turkey, and then introduced several interest rate caps on credits to selected constituencies, a government incursion into credit policy that overtly undermines the principle of central bank independence. Even more controversially, in its disinflationary efforts, the MNB resuscitated one of the pre-Orbán strategies that it had fought hard to unravel: enlisting foreign finance by offering high returns on short-term inflows into central bank instruments. Orbán had promised Hungarians a new macrofinancial contract that reduced the distributional benefits accruing to foreign finance from its large footprint in banking and capital markets, including sovereign bond markets (Ban and Bohle, 2021; Gabor, 2010). Instead, Orbán's illiberal state focused on articulating a new state-capital relationship that prioritized the growth of local, regime-friendly capitalists, national ownership of finance alongside a continued reliance on multinational corporations.

This paper unpacks the macrofinancial aspects of illiberal state-capital relationships emerging in post-neoliberal polities. A macrofinancial lens is useful to scrutinize the claim that the Orbán regime is a paradigmatic case of 'authoritarian developmentalism', where a strong state can bend local capital to the strategic priorities of the authoritarian rulers (see Arsel et al., 2021), often by using regime-controlled financial institutions as disciplinary instruments. Paradoxically, this paper argues that Hungary did not go far enough in setting up institutions that could coerce private capital into pursuing the strategic priorities of the state. Rather, Hungary's efforts to build a local capitalist block closely mirror a new state-capital nexus emerging in post-2008 liberal democracies, whereby the state's increasingly expansive ambitions – regarding decarbonization or industrial policy, for instance – do not rely on public investment and ownership, but instead on crowding in private capital through an 'incentives, not regulations' approach that leaves the pace and path of transformation largely at the discretion of private capital. The critical macrofinance literature conceptualizes this return of the state in post-neoliberalism as the 'de-risking state' (see Gabor, 2020, 2023; Dutta et al., 2020). Hungary can be conceptualized as a paradigmatic case of autocratic de-risking: a state that seeks to build up local capital through market-based credit instruments, both via banks and bond markets, rather than through close, strategic control of credit flows and other institutional mechanisms for disciplining private capital. To put it simply, Hungary was not authoritarian enough in its approach towards local and foreign capital when the rise of inflationary pressures demanded it because the state did not have 'authoritarian' macrofinancial institutions that could be tailored towards effective price controls. Instead, a central bank in overt conflict with the government returned to the anti-inflationary practices of the financial capitalism period – and to that period's contested distributional politics that disproportionately benefitted foreign finance.

This paper identifies two distinctive periods in the Orbán regime's macrofinancial politics. In the first pre-inflationary period, the Hungarian Central Bank played a key role in the autocratic de-risking project to reverse decades of dependent financialization, replacing it with financial nationalism (Johnson and Barnes, 2015) and a new distributional politics that shrank the presence of foreign financial capital. In the second period, during the COVID-19 shock and extended inflationary pressures throughout 2022, the MNB reverted to pre-Orbán dependent financialization, undermining a key pillar of Orbánomics. The MNB raised interest rates and offered investors, both local and foreign, substantive profit opportunities through its own deposit facilities to attract capital inflows and engineer a currency appreciation. This triggered an overt conflict with the Orbán government over the contractionary impulses in the MNB's interest and credit policies, culminating in the European Central Bank (ECB) criticizing Orbán's government for its attacks on central bank independence.[1]

From dependent financialization to autocratic de-risking

Scholarly analyses of illiberalism frame questions of autocratic durability through the willingness of foreign/domestic capital to re/invest (Camba and Epstein, 2023). This applies well to Hungary's relationship with multinational corporations (MNCs). The Orbán regime secured MNCs' investment, employment, and public relations in exchange for low corporate income taxes (at 9% flat rate, the lowest in Europe in 2022) and other substantive (tax) subsidies. In this area, Orbán preserved the previous liberal approach of aggressively encouraging Foreign Direct Investments (FDIs) through tax incentives, low corporate taxes, weak labor standards, and low wages that created an enclave economy.

The regime made a substantive break with the past in seeking to redirect Hungarian capitalism away from its dependence on global finance (Piroska, 2022; Sebok and Simons, 2022). Orbán came to power in 2010, as

---

1   'ECB says Hungary government decree has impaired central bank independence', *Reuters*, 26 April 2023: https://www.reuters.com/world/europe/ecb-says-hungary-govt-decree-has-impaired-cenbank-independence-2023-04-26/

Hungary' regime of dependent financialization was in a profound crisis. Orbán pointed to the distributional politics he had inherited and intended to overturn: foreign financial capital dominated banking and capital markets, leaving Hungary and other Eastern European countries vulnerable to downturns in the global dollar financial cycle, and forcing the cost of crises onto Hungarian citizens and businesses (Gabor, 2010; Ban and Bohle, 2021). In part, this distributional set-up had been deliberately supported by central banks, which relied on capital inflows to achieve disinflation targets. Because inflation rates reflected exchange rate dynamics, the fastest disinflation strategy, deployed systematically across Central Europe, was to engineer exchange rate appreciations. In the absence of large trade surpluses that could strengthen the currency, central banks developed instruments to attract capital inflows into local currency assets, such as central bank bonds, sovereign bonds or equity[2] (Gabor, 2010). But in 2008, a sudden stop in capital inflows after the collapse of Lehman Brothers triggered a rapid currency depreciation, leaving mortgage holders or small and medium-sized enterprises (SMEs) indebted in foreign currencies (euros, Japanese yen, or Swiss francs) with the burden of higher interest rates and a weaker Hungarian forint (HUF), pressures that were then exacerbated by the austerity imposed through International Monetary Fund (IMF) policies.

Orbán's government set out to overturn the distributional advantages enjoyed by foreign financial capital by shrinking its footprint in the Hungarian financial system. In 2012, Orbán proposed to 'create a new economic system: a significant ambition….part of the new model is to have 50% of the banking system in Hungarian hands'[3].

The Orbán regime imposed special bank levies and sectoral taxes, forcing banks to assume some of the burden of foreign currency (FX) loans that had previously been entirely left to households and small businesses.

2   The MNB issued its own carry-trade vehicles, offering foreign investors access to its risk-free HUF deposits, while simultaneously accommodating foreign banks' strategies to supplement returns by extending mortgage and consumer loans in foreign currencies, predominantly in Swiss francs and euros.

3   'The Bank of Viktor Orbán', *Financial Times*, 29 May 2022: https://www.ft.com/content/f9ba0f39-429d-4d9d-bd2e-fb78b363dfe4

Hungary also de facto nationalized the 18 private pension funds in the country by ceasing state contributions for citizens choosing to continue with a private pension. By 2015, domestic ownership of banking assets increased to 60%, with two of the country's largest three banks owned by Orbán's political allies (Oellerich, 2019, pp. 39–55). Banks were forced to convert foreign currency (euros, Swiss francs, and Japanese yen) mortgage loans, and then personal and car loans, into local currency. These measures, by far the most comprehensive structural reforms in financial systems across Eastern Europe, were paired with a consistent commitment to achieving and maintaining fiscal surpluses (Matolcsy and Palotai, 2018).

Alongside financial reform, the Orbán government sought to align the MNB more closely with its priorities. Under pressure from European institutions, the government quickly abandoned its early institutional reforms that would have curtailed MNB's independence[4], and instead placed Matolcsy, an ally, in charge of the bank. Matolcsy's task – to turn recession into growth – would, in his words, be possible 'because the central bank's leadership will be the number one strategic partner of the government'.[5]

This strategic partnership – conceptualized here as autocratic de-risking – was built upon two pillars: (a) credit policies to increase lending to local capitalists (particularly SMEs), and (b) increasing state autonomy from foreign finance.

Building a national capitalist class though autocratic de-risking

The scholarly accounts of Hungary's increased assertiveness regarding credit policy typically connect the growing domestic and state ownership of banking to preferential loans that consolidate the political legitimacy and economic power of the elites supporting the government (Piroska, 2020). Bank loans to Orbán associates were used to acquire control of commercial media or privatized universities.

4   https://ec.europa.eu/commission/presscorner/detail/en/IP_12_803
5   Krisztina Than and Sandor Peto, 'Orban to use Hungary central bank in battle for growth', *Reuters*, 10 January 2013: https://www.reuters.com/article/uk-hungary-cbank-insight-idUKBRE9090TF20130110

But such instances of political-driven lending should not be confused with a developmentalist credit policy or authoritarian developmentalism (Artsel et al., 2021). Rather, these mask a broader reliance on autocratic de-risking: supporting local capitalists through market-based credit instruments. In contrast, the (authoritarian) developmental states of East Asia deployed both credit policy for strategic industrial upgrading and state-controlled finance as a tool to push local capital towards industrial priorities (Onis, 1991), understood as the nurturing of local firms 'across a broad range of major global industries, capable of acting as first-tier suppliers to multinational corporations and even competing head-to-head with them' (Wade, 2018, p. 525).

Take the Hungarian Central Bank's Funding for Growth Scheme (FGS). Through its various iterations, the FGS offers a powerful example of authoritarian de-risking, modelled after the Bank of England's 2012 Funding for Lending Scheme[6]. Introduced in 2013, the FGS first aimed to increase bank lending to SMEs (see Figure 1). The MNB offered banks refinancing loans at 0%, which the banks could access on the condition that their SME loan portfolio increased, at a maximum of 2.5% interest, for several activities: fixed capital formation, working capital acquisition, FX loan refinancing and prefinancing of EU funds. Cheaper wholesale funding for banks (from the MNB) would translate into cheaper retail funding for SMEs.[7] The sectoral composition across the multiple FGS schemes between 2013 and 2021 shows concentration in trade/repair, agriculture, and real estate, but less so in manufacturing. Why is this a monetary de-risking approach? The MNB seeks to mobilize private investment by changing the risk/return profile of those investments, but without performance criteria attached to preferential credit, or even a well-designed sectoral allocation strategy. It leaves private investments at the discretion of local capital, which remains in the driving seat. This is not state-led capitalism, as the state – in this case the central bank – does not dictate the quantity of private investment, nor does it target productivity-improving sectors. For this, the state would have imposed performance criteria, and introduced

---

6 https://www.bankofengland.co.uk/-/media/boe/files/quarterly-bulletin/2012/the-funding-for-lending-scheme.pdf

7 https://www.mnb.hu/letoltes/nhp-tanulma-nyko-tet-2022-eng-0923.pdf

other institutional tools to deploy finance as an instrument of compelling local capitalists to support its strategic priorities. Instead, the 'strategic partnership' between the government and the central bank was not particularly concerned with *the type* of local capitalists that received support.

Figure 1: Sectoral Distribution of the Funding for Growth Schemes, 2013–2021

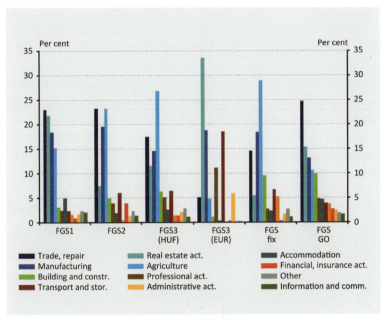

Note: by contract amount. The sectoral distribution does not include sole proprietors, but primary agricultural producers are includedas part of the agricultural sector.
Source: Central Credit Information System, MNB
(https://www.mnb.hu/en/statistics/statistical-data-and-information)

In this sense, the illiberal reliance on de-risking private credit flows suggests that Orbánomics did not set out to build a 'conservative developmentalism' but rather a 'national-neoliberalism' (Ban et al., 2021). Compare this with the capital-state relationship established by Korea's authoritarian regime: the state exercised close control over the local firms in strategic industries it chose to support (with preferential credit and other subsidies), ruthlessly penalizing poor performers and only rewarding good performers (with criteria built, for instance, on export targets) through a complex institutional architecture of coercion that included close control over the flow of credit through state-owned banks, limits to market entry to promote economies of scale, price controls to curb monopoly power (of as much as 110 commodities, including strategic inputs for industrial sectors), and capital controls to prevent elite rent-seeking (Amsden, 1992).

Green lending policies were also organized through the de-risking logic of 'carrots without sticks' (Dafermos et al., 2021). Under a sustainability mandate implemented in 2021, the MNB introduced green funding for housing and engaged in purchasing green mortgage bonds, *without* penalties for dirty credit. In contrast, the European Central Bank's strategy to decarbonize monetary policy developed a framework to tilt the corporate bond portfolio from dirty to green issuers, which, in practice, rewarded good climate performers and penalized bad performers. For instance, the FGS Green Home Programme offered up to HUF 200 billion at 0% wholesale financing to lenders to incentivize green housing mortgages at 2.5% maximum interest rates. According to IMF estimates, subsidized bank lending through both the MNB and government schemes increased to around 30% of total bank credit to non-financial corporates, and 44% for SMEs (Lybek, 2023). Again, these green loans were not accompanied by institutional mechanisms to regularly monitor the carbon footprint of the issuers.

Thus, autocratic regimes do not necessarily follow the developmentalist path even with increased control of domestic credit institutions. Rather, the illiberal Hungarian regime preserved the pre- Orbán strategy of aggressively courting MNCs with incentives[8]: between 2010 and 2016, domestic capital received less than one-quarter of the total subsidies, with the bulk directed towards foreign manufacturing – eight of the top ten recipients were foreign car manufacturers (Camba and Epstein, 2023). This changed little after the COVID-19 shock, as Hungary preserved one of the most generous regimes of subsidies for foreign capital[9].

[8] For instance, in 2014 Hungary allocated 1.63% of its GDP to subsidies, while the EU average stood at 0.72%.

[9] This includes a favorable group taxation regime that allows company group members to offset up to 50% of other group members' negative tax bases (or previous group tax losses): https://www.pwc.com/hu/en/kiadvanyok/assets/pdf/Invest-in-Hungary-2022.pdf

The 2008 global financial crisis raised difficult questions for Eastern European countries that had built their banking systems around foreign ownership, often through fire-sale privatizations accompanying shock therapy. Before Lehman's collapse, high levels of foreign bank ownership led to systemic vulnerabilities as large cross-border banking loans supported foreign-currency lending, which in turn amplified consumption, housing booms, and current account deficits (Gabor, 2010). Three of the most vulnerable countries – Hungary, Romania and Latvia – were forced to request IMF emergency loans in 2008–2009.

But the post-Lehman implosion was not entirely market made. Rather, central banks across the region had actively sought to deepen their countries' reliance on foreign finance, making it key to disinflation efforts where other monetary/fiscal or structural instruments to reduce inflation were (politically) unavailable. With post-socialist governments hesitant to deploy price controls, often because of external neoliberal pressure, central banks had to engineer exchange rate appreciations that would lower prices, given substantive exchange rate pass into prices through across the region – that is, because of substantial import dependence, local prices are highly responsive to exchange rate movements, with depreciations quickly reflected in higher prices and vice versa. Such central bank engineering took the form of encouraging carry trades and leveraged borrowing in low-yielding currencies (US dollars, euros, Japanese yen) to invest in countries with higher interest rates in Eastern Europe and elsewhere (Galati et al., 2007).

Thus, central banks used their liquidity frameworks to de-risk local currency assets for carry traders, including local (foreign-owned) banks and non-resident investors. Typically, this involved offering sterilization instruments, as central banks issued debt instruments – securities or short-term deposits – to carry traders. Foreign owned banks in Eastern Europe turned this into sterilization games: they borrowed USD or EUR from parent banks/international money markets, sold these to local central banks, and either placed the local currency proceeds in central bank debt or lent them to non-resident investors, who in turn purchased local government bonds (Christensen, 2004; Gabor, 2010). De-risking structurally entangled the state and foreign finance: central banks could meet their inflation mandate, while Ministries of Finance saw their borrowing costs reduced.

By 2011, when Orbán assumed power, the MNB had issued around 11% of Hungary's GDP in 2-week MNB bills for sterilization (see Figure 2)[10]. The MNB used bills to attract capital inflows, issuing an attractive, liquid carry trade asset for both local banks and non-resident investors, who financed their 6.5% MNB bills with EUR funding at 0.25% rates. As Figure 2 illustrates, MNB bills accounted for 33% of its liabilities, higher than currency in circulation (22%) or commercial bank reserves (4%), and substantively higher than emerging economy averages at around 16% in 2011. Put differently, the MNB dedicated more of its balance sheet to bribing carry traders into supporting disinflation than to traditional activities like issuing currency or supporting the interbank payment system.

Figure 2: The Structure of Central Bank Liabilities for Selected Countries

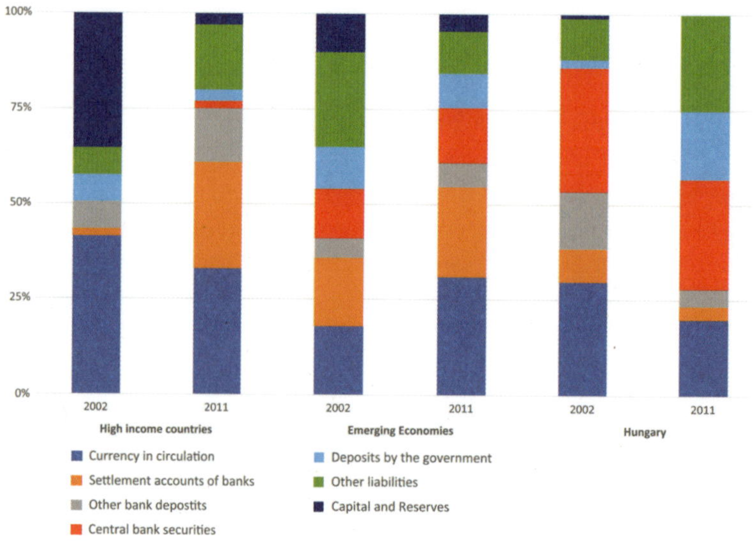

- Currency in circulation
- Settlement accounts of banks
- Other bank depostits
- Central bank securities
- Deposits by the government
- Other liabilities
- Capital and Reserves

Source: MNB (https://www.mnb.hu/en/statistics/statistical-data-and-information)

10   See https://www.mnb.hu/letoltes/erhart-kicsak-kuti-molnar-monostori.pdf

In distributional terms, the MNB validated and amplified the profitability of foreign finance, directly through carry trade sterilizations, and indirectly by encouraging local banks to prioritize short-term market activities at the expense of long-term relationship lending to local capital.

The systemic vulnerabilities of state dependency on foreign finance came into sharp focus after the Lehman collapse. Foreign ownership of HUF sovereign bonds fell significantly as foreign investors dumped sovereign bonds to protect carry returns (see Figure 3), intensifying pressures on the exchange rate. Parent banks threatened to withdraw cross-border loans to subsidiaries, seeking to prop up their own balance sheets, vulnerable to the European Banking crisis. The 2008 IMF Stand-by Arrangement and the European Bank Coordination 2009 Vienna Initiative sought to protect the increasingly controversial distributional status quo.

Figure 3: Foreign Ownership of Hungarian Sovereign Debt, Local and Foreign Currencies (2007–2022)

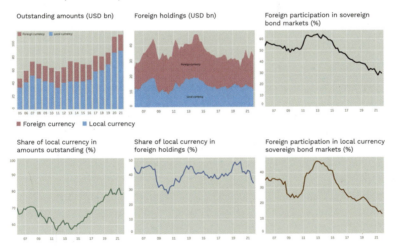

Source: Bank for International Settlements (BIS) data

Under Matolcsy's leadership, the MNB sought to radically change the distributional politics of the central bank through its 2014 Self-Financing Programme. This involved three interventions: a) shift government bond issuance to local currency; b) reduce dependency on foreign demand for sovereign debt; and c) change the central bank's liquidity management to both reduce dependency on carry trades and shift commercial bank demand from sterilization instruments to HUF sovereign bonds.

In cooperation with the Government Debt Management Agency (ÁKK), local currency sovereign debt in total outstanding increased from under 60% in 2014 to around 80% in 2021. In this approach, the MNB followed the G20 Local Currency Bond Market Initiative that advocated for local currency bonds to improve the ability of developing countries to withstand volatile capital inflows. Having nationalized private pension funds, the MNB sought to foment local bank demand for HUF sovereign bonds. To do this, it reoriented liquidity management towards shifting the carry trade activities of banks to the HUF sovereign segment and broader lending to the real economy. The central bank first replaced its main sterilization instrument, the 2-week MNB bills, with a two-week deposit, a less liquid instrument that carry traders could not easily trade. It then extended the term, reduced the issuance frequency, and capped the volume of sterilization deposits (see Figure 4), seeking to 'crowd out excess bank liquidity' from the central bank policy instrument into HUF sovereign bonds:

> *By crowding excess bank liquidity out of the policy instrument, the steps described above are expected to facilitate a decline in market yields. Having been crowded out, excess liquidity may flow into the interbank market and into the government securities market beside the Bank's other deposit instruments; therefore, the resulting interest rate effect is likely to arise in these sub-markets, supporting the Bank's schemes to stimulate bank lending and the Self-Financing Programme.*
> MNB (2020: 12)

In sum, the authoritarian shift in Eastern Europe set out to overturn the distributional politics of the previous liberal regimes, which had benefitted foreign capital, without a radical shift in the structural logic of state interventions focused on mobilizing private capital into policy priorities. Orbán promised a new economic system and delivered in as far as it shrank the distributional benefits for foreign finance. But the system failed to dismantle the old growth model because it essentially preserved the old tools of de-risking: along with aggressive subsidies for MNCs, the most notable policy interventions saw the MNB swapping the beneficiaries of its de-risking from foreign carry traders to local capital, organizing interventions to encourage higher lending to local capitalists or middle-class households (for instance, mortgage lending) and, simultaneously, higher private demand for HUF sovereign bonds.[11]

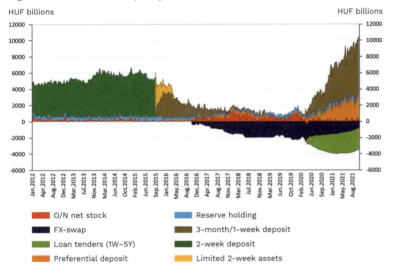

Figure 4: Selected MNB Liquidity Instruments, 2012–2021

Source: MNB

In parallel, businessmen with ties to the Orbán regime set up a large network of private equity funds through which they took ownership of Hungarian assets. Private equity funds raise capital from accredited investors, like pension funds, and qualified clients, like high net-worth

---

11   The COVID-19 pandemic saw the MNB adopting a range of unconventional policies from the de-risking toolkits of other European central banks (Gabor, 2023), including unconventional sovereign and corporate bond purchases alongside an extension of the FGS.

individuals, and invest on their behalf. Private equity funds can invest in companies or infrastructure assets, typically through an aggressive approach that seeks to maximize short-run profits. But profits are not the only attraction for investors in private equity funds; secrecy also plays an important role, as private equity funds are not subject to public disclosure requirements. Recent reports[12] suggest that private equity funds owned by close Orbán associates have controlling stakes in Magyar Bankholding (MBH), the superbank that the Orbán regime intends to deploy as a national development bank, as well as in large food and manufacturing companies, and a substantive portfolio of infrastructure assets, including hotel chains, properties in Budapest, recycling plants, highways, and camping sites.

A radically different institutional arrangement would have involved the MNB directly targeting sovereign yields or deploying credit policies as an instrument to push (local) capitalists into adopting state priorities when market conditions changed. The pitfalls of this strategy would become apparent with the global inflationary pressures in the wake of the COVID-19 pandemic.

Inflationary struggles undermining autocratic de-risking

Inflation in Hungary accelerated to its highest level in decades starting in early 2021. From 2.7% year-on-year in January 2021, it peaked at 24.5% in December 2022 (see Figure 5.1). As in other European countries, external shocks played an important part, including COVID-related supply chain disruptions and the surge in commodity prices, primarily energy and food, further amplified by Russia's war in Ukraine. For instance, the cost of imported energy more than doubled within a year, with the overall imported energy bill reaching around 10% of GDP in 2022. But specific domestic circumstances – related to the fault lines of the autocratic de-risking strategy to build a national bourgeoisie – are important to understanding why Hungary's inflation was the highest in the EU, nearly double the EU average, and well above regional peers.

12 https://www.direkt36.hu/en/oriasi-vagyonokat-rejtettek-el-kormanykozeli-korok-de-most-egy-hivatalos-adatbazis-leleplezte-oket/

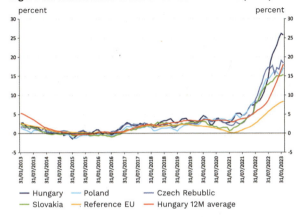

Figure 5.1: Harmonized Index of Consumer Prices (HICP)

Figure 5.2: Exchange Rates (Feb. 2019=100)

Note: HUF=Hungarian forint, PLN=Polish złoty, CZK=Czech koruna, RON=Romanian leu, EUR=euro
Source: MNB (https://www.mnb.hu/en/statistics/statistical-data-and-information)

First, Hungary saw a faster and sharper exchange rate depreciation throughout 2021 and particularly throughout 2022. By October 2022, the HUF had depreciated by nearly 40% on 2019 values, significantly more than currencies in Poland or Romania, and in stark contrast with Czechia, whose currency appreciated (see Figure 5.2). Against tighter global financial conditions, Hungary-specific dynamics included a widening current account deficit led by expensive energy imports, and disputes with the EU that added to risk perceptions, intensifying pressure on the exchange rate and imported inflation. Indeed, the European Commission notified Hungary that it was considering the suspension of EU disbursements to Hungary for breaches of the principles of the rule of law in April 2022, and by December 2022 the European Council agreed to withhold EUR 6.3 billion in budgetary commitments[13], roughly a third of the Hungarian government's outstanding foreign currency debt.

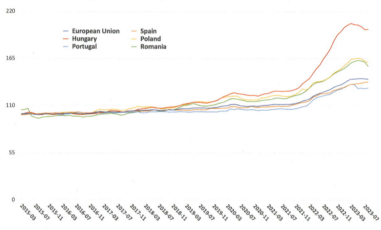

Figure 6: Food Harmonized Indices of Consumer Prices, Selected Countries, 2022–June 2023 (June 2015=100)

Source: Eurostat

Second, food prices rose at the fastest pace in the EU, despite selective price controls introduced in February 2022 (see Figure 6). Processed food prices contributed the most to the rise in core inflation. An unusually severe drought, the Russian invasion of Ukraine, and depreciating exchange rates that increased the price of imported food all played an important role, amplified by the sellers' responses to price controls: in a bid to preserve margins, distributors and retailers raised prices on other products. The Hungarian state's attempts to design and implement effective price

13   https://www.consilium.europa.eu/en/press/press-releases/2022/12/12/rule-of-law-conditionality-mechanism/

controls were thus ineffective, in part because the autocratic de-risking approach paid little attention to creating state institutions that could compel local capital to adopt strategic state priorities.

Table 1: Price Controls at Sectoral Level, Hungary

	Coverage	Description	Cost borne by
Household utility price	2014–	All households	Prices of household gas and electricity fixed at around 24 and 75 euros per MWh, respectively, for all levels of consumption. In August 2022, the cap was increased for consumption above the national average to price levels closer to market rates, which are to be adjusted quarterly.	Utility companies and government
Motor fuels price	Nov. 15, 2021 to Dec. 6, 2022	Resident privately-owned vehicles, taxis and agricultural machinery	Price of petrol and diesel capped at HUF 480 per liter (EUR 1.3 euros at 11/15/21 exchange rate). Coverage was initially universal, then narrowed to residents only in July 2022. The cap had been extended twice to end-2022, but eventually ended earlier than planned as it led to supply pressure and closures of petrol stations.	Wholesalers
Food price cap	Feb. 2022 to Apr. 30, 2023	Universal	Prices of granulated sugar, wheat flour, sunflower oil, pork leg, chicken breast, and 2.8% cow milk capped at their 10/15/21 levels. The cap has been extended several times, and the list was expanded in November 2022 to include potatoes and eggs capped at end-September retail price.	Retailers
Mortgage interest	Jan. 2022 to mid-2023	Variable rate mortgages, and those with fixation dates through June 2023	Mortgage rates capped until June 30, 2023 at October 27, 2021 levels for mortgages with short- to medium-term interest fixation periods. Analysts estimate that capped mortgages amount to about 2.3 percent of GDP or 22.7 percent of own funds (total bank lending for housing purchases was 8.1 percent of GDP at end-August 2022).	Banks
SME interest	Nov. 15, 2022 to Jun. 30, 2023	All SMEs with variable interest-rate loans	Interest rates on HUF-denominated business loans to SMEs capped at the reference rate as of June 28, 2022. The MNB estimates the cost to banks at about 0.1 percent of GDP.	Banks
Large deposits interest	Nov. 21, 2022 to Mar. 31, 2023	Large depositors with at least HUF 20mn in deposits	Interest rates on some large deposits capped at the average 3-month T-bill yield. The government's objective is to divert those funds toward government securities.	Large depositors (foregone interest)
Student loan interest	Jan. 2023–	Student loans	The interest rate on student loans that are subject to interest will stay at 4.99 percent as of January 2023, when it would otherwise have increased to 10 percent for 100,000 borrowers. Other student loans are interest free.	State-owned student loan provider

Source: IMF Country Report (February 2023), p. 6 (https://www.imf.org/-/media/Files/Publications/CR/2023/English/1HUNEA2023002.ashx)

Price controls went beyond food items, as the IMF (2023) reports in detail (see Table 1). Their faulty design had significant macroeconomic consequences, forcing the government into abrupt U-turns that fed inflationary dynamics. Take motor fuel. Initially, the government imposed a cap well below market prices (November 2021), in an attempt to contain the passthrough onto consumer retail prices. As foreign companies cut fuel shipments, the state-owned Hungarian gas and oil company MOL struggled to meet demand, resulting in shortages, queues, and a critical supply condition. The government then abruptly lifted the cap in December 2022, which in turn generated an additional inflationary impulse, as fuel prices jumped by 27% year-over-year and contributed close to 2 percentage points to Consumer Price Index (CPI) headline inflation year-over-year that month. This exacerbated the inflationary dynamics of the August 2022 decision to lift price caps on household energy utility closer to market rates.

By April 2023, the Orbán government scaled up efforts to preserve the legitimacy of its authoritarian rule. First, it extended price controls to 20 basic food categories, in parallel with measures to force retailers to cut prices of at least one item in each group. Second, it set out to build new institutions to discipline capital: it announced a state-backed price monitoring system that could push businesses towards disinflation, traditionally a mark of developmentalism. But the political will to transition from autocratic de-risking to developmentalism proved short-lived. In June 2023, the government announced it planned to terminate all food price controls beginning in August 2023, while its online price monitoring system[14] – designed in a joint working group involving the Ministry for Economic Development, the Competition Authority, the Ministry of Agriculture, the Central Statistical Office, the Ministry of Justice, and the Consumer Protection Authority (formed in March 2023) – shifted the disciplinary tools from the state to the market. Consumers were to use it as a transparency tool to make informed purchase decisions.

The Hungarian government's mishandling of the price caps – a reflection of international supply conditions as well as the weakening of its ability to preserve strategies of autocratic hedging – exacerbated inflationary pressures. It also forced a tightening of both monetary and fiscal

14 John Woods, 'Hungary's brand new price monitoring system kicked off: here is how it works', *Daily News Hungary*, 7 February 2023: https://dailynewshungary.com/hungarys-brand-new-price-monitoring-system-kicked-off-here-is-how-it-works/

conditions and set the stage for an overt conflict with the central bank, which was advocating for a return to the strategies and distributional politics of the neoliberal era.

Figure 7.1: Central Bank Rates and 3-Month Interbank Rates in the Region

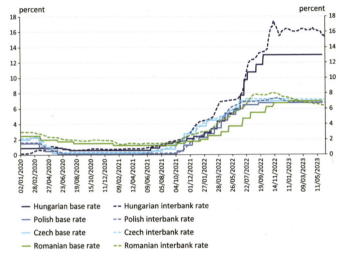

Figure 7.2: 10-year Government Bond Spreads, Selected Countries

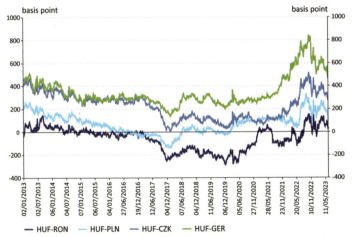

Source: MNB (https://www.mnb.hu/en/statistics/statistical-data-and-information)

On the monetary side, the MNB started to raise policy rates from mid-2021. By mid-2023, the base rate (the policy rate of the central bank) was around 15%, nearly double the regional average (see Figure 7.1). Interbank interest rates also increased substantively, as the MNB returned to pre-Orbán carry-trade strategies in October 2022 (see more in the next section). Fearing the impact on the housing market and the legitimacy of the regime, the Orbán government decided to intervene directly in credit policy, overstepping into the formal domain of the central bank. The government introduced several price controls on credit products, capping mortgage rates, SME interest rates, and student loan rates (see Table 1).

Figure 8: Budget Deficits as Share of GDP, 1995–2023

Source: IMF statistics (https://www.imf.org/external/datamapper/G_X_G01_GDP_PT@FM/HUN)

Borrowing conditions also tightened for the government. The spreads between 10-year Hungarian government bonds and German, Polish and Czech bonds increased throughout 2022 (see Figure 7.2). By end of 2022, Hungary's borrowing costs were higher than Romania's, reversing the historical trend of the preceding five years. In part, this reflected the MNB's decision to taper outright purchases of government bonds, unwinding its unconventional monetary policy measures. At the same time, the Hungarian government decided against substantively reversing the loose fiscal stance of the COVID-19 pandemic before the April 2022 elections (see Figure 8). The May 2022 announcement of windfall taxes on banks, insurers, large retail chains, the energy industry and trading firms, telecom companies, and airlines, intended to cover the costs of energy price caps (and military expenditures), did little to return the intra-year negative cash balance of the central government towards 2021 levels. The fiscal stance tightened by 2023, to an estimated 5.4% of GDP, driven by lower-than-expected revenues generated by the overall demand shock affecting the Hungarian economy. By May 2023, Hungary entered a technical recession, as demand for imports shrank at the fastest pace in a decade, in tandem with net lending. The ability of Orbánomics to deliver to its constituencies was increasing questioned, not just by trade unions and small business owners, but also by former political allies.

The Matolcsy U-turn: Questioning Orbánomics, and back to the distributional politics of financial capitalism

> *The government has not found the keys...we cannot overcome this energy price explosion and inflation crisis in the old ways... communism already showed that price caps don't work...the system collapsed, let's not return to it with such techniques.*
> György Matolcsy, MNB governor, January 2023[15]

It is worth remembering that one key pillar of Orbánomics sought to untie Hungarian capitalism from global finance. This would weaken the infrastructural power of finance (Braun, 2020) and, perhaps more importantly, reckon 'with the role of capital in underpinning contemporary political and economic structures' (Sebok and Simmons, 2022 p.12). The strategic alliance between the central bank and the government would play a key role, with the central bank seeking to untie its monetary policy operations from carry traders, which were viewed as destabilizing instruments of financial dependency. The very first measures taken by the Matolscy-led MNB sought to create local demand for HUF sovereign bonds by pushing foreign investors out of MNB instruments.

---

15   'Hungary's soaring inflation puts squeeze on Viktor Orbán', *Financial Times*, 28 January 2023: https://www.ft.com/content/6074bbc2-247b-46a1-bcce-03c464cec8b4

But the COVID-19 shock and inflationary pressures combined with the failure of outright price controls saw the MNB return to the techniques of financialized dependency. The bank opened access to investment funds and to its growing range of unconventional instruments, such as the Bond Funding for Growth Scheme (BFG) and the government securities purchase program, and to its collateralized loans. It also expanded the range of eligible collateral to include investment shares of HUF securities and real estate funds.

Figure 9: Selected Assets and Liabilities of the MNB

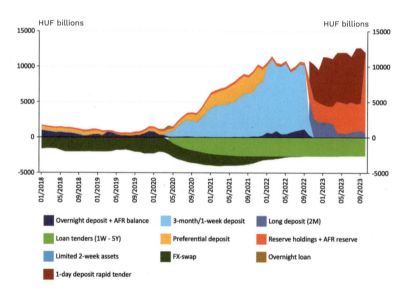

Source: MNB (https://www.mnb.hu/en/statistics/statistical-data-and-information)

The more controversial move came in an emergency decision on October 17, 2022, as the Hungarian forint was rapidly depreciating. The MNB introduced a one-day deposit facility paying investors an 18% interest rate, well-above the official 13% policy rate, and held deposit tenders daily – effectively bribing both local and foreign investors to scale up carry-trade inflows into its deposit facility, reviving the liberal de-risking strategy it had deployed throughout the pre-Orbán years. By February 2023, the MNB was attracting around USD 45 billion in one-day deposits, rewarded at an 18% annual interest rate, and a smaller volume in MNB Discount Bills (see Figure 9). Ironically, while Matolscy was publicly denouncing the government for returning to 'communist' practices of price controls (conveniently ignoring their widespread use in capitalist countries after WWII), it quietly returned to the liberal practices of attracting investors for MNB instruments to defend the exchange rate and ease inflationary pressures.

Historically, authoritarian regimes often chose to preserve or even strengthen central bank independence. Independent central banks can pursue disinflationary policies while shielding the government from the associated political backlash, and, equally important, can protect a pro-capital distributional status quo that benefits capital owners closely associated with ruling elites (Aklin et al., 2022). But not all authoritarian regimes evolve alike. Before the COVID-19 pandemic, the MNB's turn to autocratic de-risking did not seek to replace the market, but rather reoriented the logic of steering private capital that once benefitted foreign finance to benefit local (small) businesses and middle-class households. In that sense, the strategic partnership with the Orbán government prioritized a different section of capital. But persistent inflation weakened that strategic partnership, prompting the MNB to return to disinflationary strategies dependent on foreign finance and igniting a conflict with the government over the distributional implications of high returns for carry traders that were hurting the economy.

This conflict with a more assertive, independent central bank took a rather unexpected turn. The Orbán government decided to intervene directly in credit and interest policy with a broad range of interest rate caps on mortgages, SMEs and student loans, and, critically, with sterilization interventions. The Orbán government sought to replicate the MNB's early strategy to crowd local demand from MNB policy instruments into government debt: it capped the interest rates on large demand deposits under a year at the average 3-month Treasury Bill (T-bill) yield in November 2022, in order to restrict big local investors and banks from depositing cash in central bank facilities or purchasing MNB bills. In response, the

ECB issued a legal opinion that the Hungarian government had infringed on the independence of the MNB under Article 130 of the Treaty on the Functioning of the European Union.[16]

Notably however, the Hungarian government quietly conceded that the techniques of dependent financialization were necessary for the disinflation strategy, by continuing to allow foreign institutional investors access to the MNB's one day deposit facility via FX swaps with Hungarian HUF lenders.

Conclusion

The macrofinancial choices and politics of illiberal regimes matter. They tell us what kind of relationship with private capital such regimes champion, and the conditions under which these relationships might threaten, rather than support, the overall legitimacy of authoritarian rule. Through this lens, the Orbán regime should be understood as an example of a weak authoritarian regime that makes capitalism profitable for multinationals and local business allies but is unable or unwilling to construct state capacity to set performance targets or broader mechanisms to force capital into strategic priorities.

---

16 https://eur-lex.europa.eu/legal-content/EN/TXT/PDF/?uri=CELEX:52023AB0010&qid=1682527131068

References

Aklin, M., Kern, A., Seddon, J., and Leng, N. (2022). Central Bank Independence in Autocracies. *Available at SSRN 4081620*.

Amsden, A. H. (1992). *Asia's next giant: South Korea and late industrialization*. Oxford University Press.

Arsel, M., Adaman, F., and Saad-Filho, A. (2021). 'Authoritarian developmentalism: The latest stage of neoliberalism?' *Geoforum* 124: 261–266.

Ban, C. and Bohle, D. (2021). 'Definancialization, financial repression and policy continuity in East-Central Europe'. *Review of International Political Economy*, 28(4): 874–897.

Ban, C., Scheiring, G., & Vasile, M. (2023). 'The political economy of national-neoliberalism'. *European Politics and Society* 24(1): 96–114.

Camba, A. and Epstein, R. A. (2023). 'From Duterte to Orbán: the political economy of autocratic hedging'. *Journal of International Relations and Development*: 1–26.

Dutta, S. J., Kremers, R., Pape, F., and Petry, J. (2020). Critical macro-finance: An introduction. *Finance and Society* 6(1): 34–44.

Gabor, D. (2010). *Central banking and financialization: A Romanian account of how Eastern Europe became subprime*. Springer.

Gabor, D. (2020). 'Critical macro-finance: A theoretical lens'. *Finance and Society* 6(1): 45–55.

Gabor, D. (2023). 'The (European) Derisking State'. *Stato e Mercato* 1(127): 53–84.

International Monetary Fund (2023). 2022 Article Iv Consultation—Press Release, Staff Report, and Statement by The Executive Director for Hungary. Available at: https://www.imf.org/-/media/Files/Publications/CR/2023/English/1HUNEA2023001.ashx

Johnson, J. and Barnes, A. (2015). 'Financial nationalism and its international enablers: The Hungarian experience'. *Review of International Political Economy* 22(3): 535–569.

Lybek, M. T. (2023). *Hungarian Monetary Policy Operations Before, During, and After the Pandemic*. International Monetary Fund.

Matolcsy, G. and Palotai, D. (2018). 'The Hungarian model: Hungarian crisis management in view of the Mediterranean way'. *Financial and Economic Review* 17(2): 5–42.

Oellerich, N. (2019). *Changing Bank Ownership Patterns in Hungary: Development, Economic Nationalism, and Political Lending*. Master's thesis submitted to Central European University, Department of Political Science.

Öniş, Z. (1991). 'The logic of the developmental state'. *Comparative Politics* 24(1): 109–126.

Piroska, D. (2022). 'Financial nationalism and democracy', in Andreas Pickel (ed.), *Handbook of Economic Nationalism*, pp. 256–274. Edward Elgar Publishing.

Sebők, M. and Simons, J. (2022). 'How Orbán won? Neoliberal disenchantment and the grand strategy of financial nationalism to reconstruct capitalism and regain autonomy'. *Socio-Economic Review* 20(4): 1625–1651.

Wade, R. H. (2018). 'The developmental state: dead or alive?' *Development and Change* 49(2): 518–546.

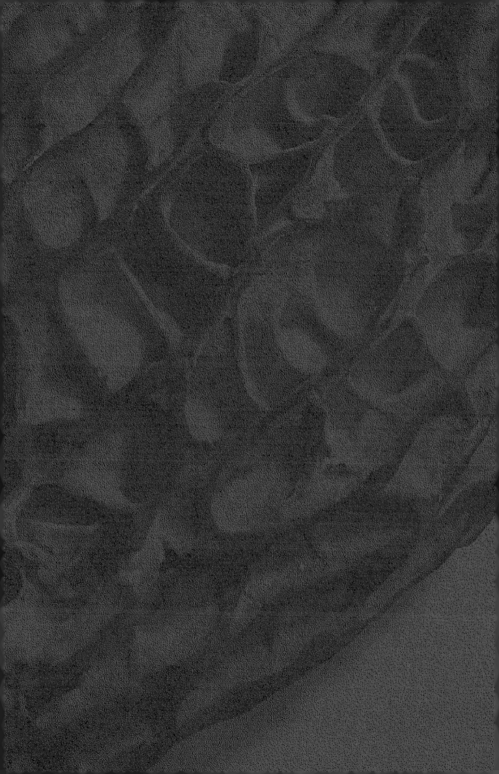

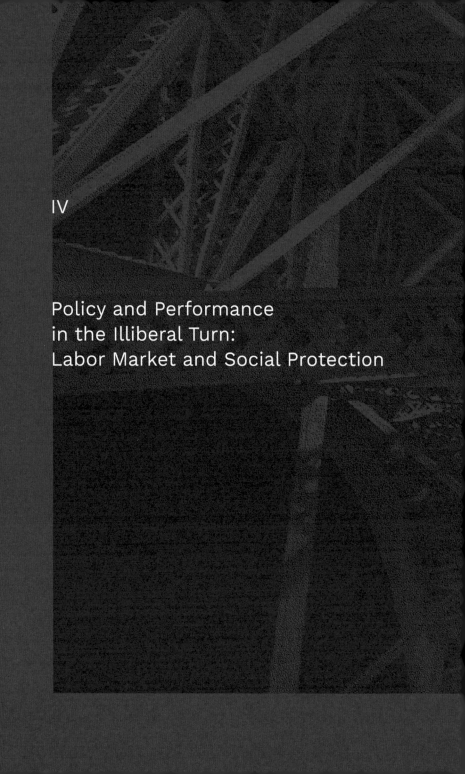

IV

Policy and Performance
in the Illiberal Turn:
Labor Market and Social Protection

The Labor and Social Policies of Neo-authoritarian Populist Governments: A Comparative Analysis of Hungary, Poland, and Türkiye

JANINE BERG
International Labour Office[1]

LUDOVICA TURSINI
The New School

The nationalist and patriarchal agendas of the governments of Hungary, Poland, and Türkiye have strong political support. But such support can be tenuous if the material conditions of its citizens is weakened or falters, and if such weakening is associated with government policy. This paper undertakes a comparative analysis of some of the main labor and social policies in Hungary, Poland, and Türkiye to understand why these governments enjoy widespread electoral support, despite an array of illiberal policies that have chipped away at the democratic foundations of the countries.

It argues that in addition to its populist rhetoric, the three governments have privileged high visibility labor and social policies that benefit the lower and middle classes that constitute the governments' political base, and which mitigate the labor market insecurity associated with the neoliberal economic model. As such, there is the seemingly contradictory tendency of the governments pursuing the flexibilization of labor rights, both individual and collective, while simultaneously delivering significant real increases in the minimum wage. Because workers typically associate their employment contracts and working conditions more generally with

[1] The views expressed in this paper are my own and do not reflect the views of the International Labour Organization.

the managerial prerogative of employers, rather than specific government policies, the regimes do not suffer the consequences of the labor flexibilization policies. And by sidelining or co-opting unions, the governments not only enable further flexibilization of the labor market, but also marginalize a potential countervailing force to the government.

Neo-authoritarianism and the suppression of countervailing forces

Fidesz in Hungary, PiS in Poland and the AKP in Türkiye have each been associated with "democratic backsliding" though to different degrees (Szikra and Oktem, 2023; Berberoglu, 2021) (see Figure 1). Part of the democratic backsliding concerns the treatment of unions, which have been marginalized in Hungary, co-opted in Poland, and attacked in Türkiye, for both economic and political objectives. With respect to economic objectives, the weakening of trade unions supports the neoliberal labor market flexibilization policies that are part of the countries' economic models, while disempowering unions helps to sideline potential political opposition to anti-democratic policies. Strong and independent unions are cornerstones of democracy (Curtis, 2021), thus policies that limit unionization, or make it less effective through restrictions on collective bargaining, ultimately weaken the working of democracies.

Figure 1: Democratic Backsliding and Regime Types

Source: Szikra and Oktem, 2023

In Hungary, Fidesz, under the leadership of Victor Orbán, came to power in 2010 when the country was still reckoning with the effects of the global financial crisis and the resulting austerity policies imposed as a condition of IMF and European Central Bank loans. The 2010 landslide victory of the Fidesz-KDNP coalition, which created a right-wing nationalist conservative alliance, allowed the government to enact drastic reforms that removed democratic guarantees from the political process (Hungler, 2022). Some of the reforms were ingrained into Cardinal Acts that can only be modified by a two-thirds majority, binding future governments to these reforms (Szikra and Öktem, 2023). The government controls, directly or indirectly through close political ties, the vast majority of print radio and television media, the result of purchases made in the late 2000s with loans from state-controlled banks (IPI, 2023). Its attacks on academic freedom culminated with the expulsion of the Central European University in 2018.[2] Judicial independence has been restricted and labor courts have been weakened. The government has been criticized for its treatment of minorities, including refugees, Roma, and LGBTQ+ people. Fidesz was a member of center-right European People's Party (EPP) but was suspended in 2021 out of concern over its commitment to democracy and the rule of law.

Unions have become marginalized under the Fidesz government. The government abandoned national tripartite bodies, including replacing the forum for national tripartite minimum-wage setting with a private sector consultation forum in 2010 (Meszmann and Szabó, 2023). The government also reduced funding to trade union confederations. In 2018, a mere 7% of the working population was unionized, most in the public sector (see Figure 2).

Poland, similar to Hungary, underwent a transition to democracy and a market economy in the early 1990s. Following a period of rapid economic growth and integration with Western Europe, it joined the European Union in 2004. In 2005, the center-right Law and Justice Party (PiS) won a narrow victory and formed a government, though it was ousted in 2007 in a vote of no confidence and replaced by a coalition

2   The Central European University moved its campus from Budapest to Vienna due to the terms of the 2017 law regulating foreign universities.

government led by the center-left Democratic Left Alliance. In the 2015 elections, PiS returned to power with a parliamentary majority and has since been accused of democratic backsliding due to dismantling of governmental checks and balances (Szikra and Öktem, 2023). In particular, the highest court in Poland does not meet EU standards of judicial independence (Smiecinska, 2021).

NSZZ Solidarność, the largest Polish trade union, has maintained close ties to the ruling PiS party, and many PiS politicians, including Jaroslaw Kaczyński, the party chairman, are former Solidarność members. The trade union has used its ties to push through popular reforms, including a lowering of the retirement age, banning Sunday trading, and curtailing the expansion of civil law contracts. It has also worked to secure increases in the minimum wage. In addition, the unions succeeded in pushing for an amendment to the Trade Union Act that expanded the eligibility for union membership to all "persons performing paid work" as a means of boosting unionization of workers on civil contracts, which are widespread in the Polish labor market (Czarzasty and Mrozowicki, 2023). The government has also supported the mining union in resisting mine closures despite the EU climate target.

Nonetheless, there has been a steady decline in unionization falling from a high of 65% (12.5 million members) in 1980 to 20% (2.6 million members) in 2000; by 2019, unionization stood at a low of 13% or 1.5 million members, 98% of whom were in the public sector (Czarzasty and Mrozowicki, 2023). Much of this decline is the result of the economic restructuring and privatization policies pursued in the 1990s, which shrunk the industrial base and led to a mass shedding of workers and, as a result, union members. However, the low unionization rate is also due to the characteristics of the industrial relations system: unionization is limited to enterprises with 10 or more employees, thereby precluding the large share (40%) of workers employed in small enterprises from unionizing. In addition, the law permits an unlimited number of unions at the workplace, leading to fragmentation, and prohibits closed shops[3]

---

3   A closed shop is an arrangement whereby a place of employment requires current membership in a specific union as a condition of employment.

(Czarzasty and Mrozowicki, 2023). Collective bargaining is limited to the enterprise level. Other features of the labor market – particularly the high share of temporary contracts and widespread use of civil contracts in employment – hurt unionization.

Figure 2: Trade Union Density and Collective Bargaining Coverage in Hungary, Poland, and Türkiye

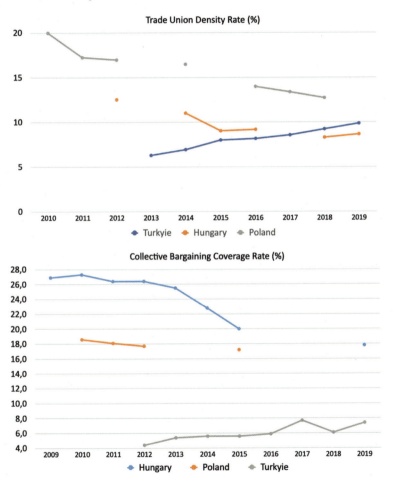

Source: ILOSTAT, International Labour Organization

While NSZZ Solidarność is independent from PiS, the close ties, both politically and ideologically, between the union and the government, and the overall weakness of the trade union movement in general, mean that unions – and particularly NSZZ Solidarność – do not act as a countervailing force to the PiS's policies.

At the furthest end of the anti-democratic spectrum is Türkiye, which shares similarities with Hungary and Poland, but has been more extreme in its pursuit of neo-authoritarianism. The Justice and Development Party (AKP) first came to power in 2002, following political and economic instability in the 1990s. Recep Tayyip Erdoğan, the party leader, served first as Prime Minister until 2014, and since then as President. During its initial years in power, the AKP adopted an ambitious sociopolitical development agenda with the aim of joining the EU; but following its landslide victory in the 2007 elections, the government became more authoritarian in its pursuit of power (Özkiziltan, 2019). In 2016, a constitutional reform was adopted that abolished the parliamentary system, removed checks and balances, and gave the president more wide-reaching powers. Following the 2016 failed coup attempt by the Gülen movement, Erdoğan instituted a state of emergency and used it to silence any remaining opposition (Kirişci and Sloat, 2019). In 2018, Erdoğan was elected President under the new constitution, and then subsequently re-elected for a second term in May 2023.

Although at first glance it appears that collective rights have strengthened in Türkiye (see Figure 2), the opposite has occurred. In 2012, the AKP promulgated a new labor law that made it easier to establish unions and be recognized for collective bargaining, but also easier for the government to curb industrial action.[4] The new law led to increased unionization in the pro-government, Hak-İş union, which was also helped by the practice of the government paying the dues for public employees (Çelik, 2015). Between 2002 and 2018, union membership in Hak-İş more than doubled from 302,000 to 654,000, whereas membership in the oldest union confederation, Türk-İş, fell from 1.95 million to 959,000, and membership in

---

[4] In particular, there are no protections against dismissal on the grounds of union membership and activity (Çelik, 2015).

DISK (Confederation of Progressive Trade Unions of Türkiye) fell from 368,000 to 161,000. The International Trade Union Confederation (ITUC) ranks Türkiye among the top 10 worst countries on its Global Rights Index, which measures the degree to which countries, and the companies that operate within them, uphold the rights of workers as outlined in international law. In 2023 it scored 5 (no guarantee of rights) as a result of the arbitrary arrest of union leaders as well as attacks on other rights; Hungary and Poland scored 3 (regular violation of rights)[5] (ITUC, 2023).

Market liberalism with labor flexibilization

The policies of the three governments towards the labor market are in line with their economic visions, which remains neoliberal. All three countries, though to varying degrees, have institutionalized the labor market precarity they inherited – or in the case of Hungary and Türkiye, have increased such precarity. At the same time, each of the governments have pursued strategic interventions in the economy that give them political leverage and support.

Hungary: The work-based society

Shortly after assuming power, in 2011, the Fidesz government adopted a new constitution that linked social rights "to a citizen's obligation to 'serve the community'". The new constitution, known as the Fundamental Law, stated that "everyone shall be obliged to contribute to the enrichment of the community through his or her work, in accordance with his or her abilities and potential."[6] Such a vision was in line with its electoral promise of creating one million new jobs by 2020 and replacing an "uncompetitive welfare state" with a "work-based society" (Szikra and Oktem, 2023, p. 7). The Fidesz government expanded the public works program (*közmunka program*) that had been instituted during the 1990s and early 2000s by the socialist government, but made it more punitive and meager, while at the

---

5   Scoring ranges from 1 (sporadic violation of rights) to 5+ (No guarantee of rights due to the breakdown of the rule of law) (ITUC, 2023).

6   Fundamental Law Article XII paragraphs (1) and (2) cited in Hungler, 2022.

same tightening unemployment benefits (Geva, 2021; Vidra, 2018). Prior to 2011, participants in the public works program earned the minimum wage. After 2011, payment was reduced to 78% of the minimum wage for full-time work, with the belief that the wage reduction would motivate participants to seek other employment. Most of the public works are low-intensive, physical tasks (drainage, cleaning sides of roads, gardening), with participants required to accept any job the municipality offers, independent of their educational level and skills. The policy aims to "activate" people and break their benefit dependency. Under the reforms, beneficiaries of unemployment insurance lose their benefits after 90 days of unemployment, unless they agree to do public works. The public works program has been criticized for being unproductive and demoralizing, with initial evaluations finding no effect on labor market insertion (Risak and Kovács, 2017). In 2016, the public works scheme employed roughly 5% of the labor force at a cost of 1% of GDP (IMF, 2017). Given its large size, it has served to decrease the unemployment rates, as participants are counted as employed.

The government's economic strategy centers on export-led manufacturing to the EU, with Hungary hosting important industrial plants of major German car and appliance manufacturers. In addition to the lowest EU corporate tax rate at 9%[7], many of the multinationals benefit from tax credits – a policy that was started under the socialist government in the 2000s but has continued under Fidesz. Between 2010 and 2020, the Hungarian government provided 770 million euros in subsidies to multinationals who in turn created 33,695 jobs (Hungler, 2022).

Moreover, its labor policies have been designed to support the needs of multinational firms. In 2018, in response to labor shortages caused by emigration, the government adopted a bill that permitted up to 400 hours of overtime and gave companies three years instead of one to pay for the work. While the measure, dubbed by the opposition as a "slave law," led to widespread protests, it nonetheless went into effect (Karasz and Kingsley, 2018). During the pandemic, the government further pursued labor market flexibilization by allowing for derogation from collective agreements.

---

7   In contrast, the highly regressive VAT is at 27%; the income tax is set at a flat rate of 15%.

It also passed a decree giving employers unilateral privileges to expand the reference period for working time banking, which had formerly been subject to collective agreement (Hungler, 2022). This measure was retained following the lifting of the state of emergency.

Despite the emphasis on private-sector-led investment, the government has been strategic in gaining hold of key industries for both economic and political purposes. The financial crisis caused havoc in the housing market as many Hungarians had mortgages denominated in Swiss francs, which were no longer affordable following the devaluation of the Hungarian forint in the fall of 2011. Orbán forced the banks to accept an artificially lowered currency exchange rate and to "shoulder the losses" making Orbán a "populist hero" (Geva, 2021, p. 83). The government then undertook an ambitious program of "financial nationalism" through a series of legal changes that made foreign ownership of some key industries unprofitable. The government was able to gain control of the banking sector, which it then used as a means to direct credit to loyalists who purchased other companies in industries of interest to the government, such as the media sector (Sebők and Simons, 2022).

Poland

Like Hungary, Poland's economic model is also highly dependent on external trade, with Poland serving, for the most part, as a low-value-added producer in German supply chains. The country has 14 special economic zones that provide tax exemptions to foreign enterprises. The emphasis on export-led growth has, for the most part, been successful as the country has sustained relatively high rates of economic growth since transition in the early 1990s, and in some areas has advanced to more value-added production (Gromada, 2023). Nevertheless, its economic model has been based on low labor costs and a flexible adjustment to demand, including through out-migration to other EU countries.

The Polish labor market is highly segmented with a disproportionate use of non-standard employment arrangements. Polish employers have relied heavily on the use of these arrangements for two decades, with the share of fixed-term contracts increasing from 2.9% in 1992 to 27.9% in 2006

(Buchner-Jeziorska, 2013). In 2018, 24% of the employed population were on fixed-term contracts, the second highest rate of temporary employment in the EU-27, just below Spain.[8] An additional 5–7% of the workforce (one to 1.4 million workers) has been hired using civil law contracts (referred to commonly in Poland as "junk contracts"), which are widespread in low-skill professions, including security guards, cleaning, and catering services (Statistics Poland, 2018).

The use of non-standard employment arrangements reflects the export-led growth strategy in place since the transition. Responding to the concerns of its electoral base, the PiS has extended some rights and benefits to workers on junk contracts[9], including pension benefits, minimum wage, and the right to unionize (Czarzasty and Mrozowicki, 2023). While commendable, it nonetheless sustains segmentation in the labor market and is less preferable than a more comprehensive solution that would root out segmentation and would involve expansion of the legal definition of employment and enforcement through labor inspections and the judiciary. Given the exceptionally low level of unionization in the private sector (2%) and the excessive use of non-standard contracts, it is not surprising that the wage share, at 46%, is the second lowest in the EU, or that it has fallen dramatically over time from 57% in 2000 and 63% in 1992 (Kalecki Foundation, n.d.).

Similar to Hungary, though less extensive, the PiS has also advocated the "rePolanization" of the economy, vowing to "stop the privatization agenda of the previous government" (Orenstein and Bugaric, 2020, p. 12). In 2016, the government imposed a special levy on the banking and insurance sectors and increased state control in this sector from 30% to over 50%. Given the importance of coal production to both the economy, its labor force, and its unions, the PiS has resisted EU climate targets, in addition to consolidating its domestic energy sector.

8   Data from Eurostat.

9   The right was granted to a specific type of civil law contract called *umowa zlecenie*. Under this contract, the contractor is required to perform a certain activity within a specified period as commissioned by the principal in return for a fixed remuneration.

Türkiye: "Authoritarian flexibilization"

In February 2001, Türkiye erupted in economic crisis following the devaluation of its exchange rate, which had previously been pegged to the dollar. The IMF provided bailout loans on the condition of a structural reform program centered on strict fiscal and monetary policies and a floating exchange rate. When the AKP assumed office in 2002, it continued with the program, and with the prospect of EU accession, Türkiye soon became the darling of financial investors, attracting substantial capital inflows in the ensuing decade, both because of the high interest rates, but also as a result of the widespread privatization program undertaken by the AKP that concerned the oil sector, transport, telecommunications, tobacco, financial services, and other industries (Szanyi, 2020).

The inflows of foreign capital and widespread privatization allowed the government to fund a massive construction spree that entailed the building of highways, busways, airports, and universities, in addition to fueling a household credit boom, with household debt rising from 2% of GDP in 2002 to 20% by 2013. The supply of new housing was facilitated by the Public Housing Authority, which was granted special privileges to direct public land towards construction through subcontracting. This not only generated rents for the government, but also allowed it to direct permits to business groups with whom it had close ties, further strengthening political support (Orhangazi and Yeldan, 2021). Construction's share of GDP, in turn, rose from 7.5% in 2004 to 17.2% by 2017 with concomitant gains in employment.

The privatization program was central to the AKP's economic vision to "create a market society", which also included flexibilization of the labor markets. In 2003, the government reformed dismissal protection such that job security would only apply to enterprises employing 30 or more workers, up from 10, while reducing severance pay. Given the importance of small and medium-sized enterprises in Türkiye, this new threshold essentially eliminated protection in all but the largest firms. The government also eased the rules on agency employment and instituted widespread outsourcing in the public sector. Between 2002 and 2011, the number of subcontracted workers increased from 358,000 to 1.5 million (Çelik, 2015).

In 2014, the government published its National Employment Strategy (NES), 2014–2023, which argued that a more flexible labor market was needed to ensure the competitiveness and efficiency of Turkish enterprises, as well as to reduce unregistered employment and high levels of youth unemployment (Ministry of Labour, 2014). Targets for the government included a better ranking in the Employing Workers component of the World Bank's Doing Business Indicators, which ranks countries (with greater labor and social security protections resulting in a lower score), in the areas of dismissal protection and severance, the use of fixed-term contracts, working hours restrictions, and the level of social security contributions ("payroll taxes"). As such, the strategy argued for the need to introduce flexible work arrangements by drafting new legislation and raising awareness among employees and employers (Ministry of Labour, 2014). The National Employment Strategy was prepared without the participation of the social partners, which is common practice but also in violation of International Labour Organization (ILO) Conventions.[10] The three main trade union confederations objected to the NES. The Confederation of Progressive Trade Unions of Turkey (DİSK) referred to it as "the most significant attack on labor rights in the history of the Republic" (Çelik, 2015, p. 626), and even the pro-government confederation Hak-İş expressed its concern. The NES was nonetheless supported wholeheartedly by the employers' organizations (Çelik, 2015). The reforms to the labor market under the AKP have been characterized by the Turkish industrial relations scholar, Aziz Çelik, as "authoritarian flexibilization", with individual labor rights being "the most unprotected in the history of the Republic", and collective labor rights and unions as the weakest in the last 50 years (Çelik, 2015).

Minimum wages: Visible and immediate

Despite the weakness and, in some instances, deterioration, in individual and collective labor rights, all three governments have been supportive of real increases in the statutory minimum wage. Between 2010 and 2019,

10   Specifically, the Tripartite Consultation (International Labour Standards) Convention, 1976 (No. 144), which Türkiye has ratified.

increases in the real value of the minimum wage have exceeded productivity growth in Hungary and Poland, and in Türkiye as well, until the inflationary crisis erased some of the gains (see Figure 3). As a result of these increases, the minimum-to-median wage ratio in all three countries is relatively high, at 63% in Poland and 71% in Hungary; in Türkiye it approaches 100% (ILO, 2020).

Figure 3: Average Annual Growth of Real Minimum Wage and Productivity, 2010–2019

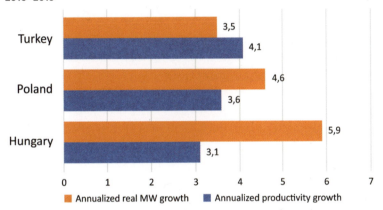

Source: ILO, 2020

While the minimum wage policy would seem to contradict the emphasis on labor competitiveness espoused by all three countries, the minimum wage nonetheless provides an important means of improving earnings among workers that can be directly associated with government policy, particularly in the absence of collective bargaining. This is particularly true in countries with one national minimum wage, which is the case in all three countries. As argued in the introduction, other labor policies, particularly concerning contractual arrangements, or weakening collective bargaining, are less visibly associated with government policies. The minimum wage is thus an important tool used by these populist governments to ensure broad electoral support, and indeed the minimum wage was raised in Türkiye just prior to the presidential election in Spring 2023.

In line with the traditional values and anti-immigration stance of the three governments, boosting fertility is a central objective, particularly in Hungary and Poland, whose fertility rates of 1.6 and 1.3 children, respectively, are well below replacement rates (Türkiye's fertility rate is 1.6), and in the case of Poland, below the EU average of 1.46 live births per woman in 2022. In addition to boosting fertility, pro-natalist social policies also seek to reinforce traditional gender roles, as they emphasize women's roles as carers (Cook, Iarskaia-Sminorva, and Kozlov, 2022; Fischer, 2020; Akkan, 2021). To support their pro-natalist, pro-family, and nationalist visions, all three countries have instituted flagship social policies that, like the minimum wage, are highly visible and benefit important swaths of the population, thus garnering electoral support. Some of the policies are also administered locally and thus reinforce clientelism (Çelik, 2015).

Hungary's earned income family tax credit

In keeping with the emphasis on work, many of the social policies in Hungary have been transformed into tax credits that are only available to the employed. In 2011, the Fidesz Party sought to boost fertility rates via the fiscal system, through the expansion of an existing earned income tax credit. The policy provides a per-child monthly allowance to be deducted from income taxes; in 2018 the credit was set at 200 euros for one child, 400 euros for two children, and 660 euros for three or more children (which, after taxes, was equivalent to a benefit of approximately 31 euros, 63 euros and 104 euros per month, respectively).[11] In addition, mothers with four or more children receive a lifelong exemption from income tax (Cook, Iarskaia-Smirnova, and Kozlov, 2022). With this policy, spending on family policy increased from 3.5% of GDP in 2010 to 6.2% of GDP in 2022. The policy is directed at middle-class families in the formal economy; participants in the public works scheme are not entitled to the deduction (Lendvai-Bainton and Szelewa, 2020; Szikra and Otkem, 2023).

11 In comparison, the average net monthly salary in Hungary in 2018 was 730 euros.

Figure 4: Fertility Rates in Hungary, Poland, and Türkiye

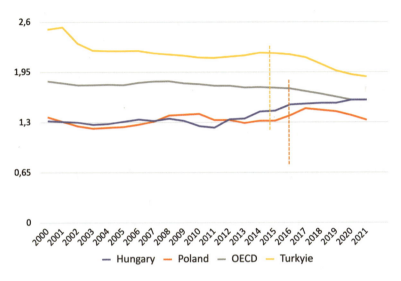

Source: World Bank

Poland's Family 500+

In 2016, the PiS introduced the Family 500+ Program with the explicit objective of boosting fertility. Initially the program provided a credit of 500ZL (120 euros) per month, per child (up to eighteen years old) to each family with two or more children or to every family with a single child if the family met the income criteria. As of mid-2019 the program was made universal, with all families, regardless of the number of children (0–17 years old) or income, receiving 500ZL credit for each child. The policy, at a cost of approximately 3% of GDP, has pushed Poland near the top for family spending in Europe (Cook et al., 2022). Family 500+ is extremely popular and contributes to the governing party's continuing success. The Family 500+ has led to a substantial reduction in child poverty (see Figure 5), though this was not the explicit intention of the program. With respect to fertility, the program led to an initial bump in fertility, but this has since tapered off (see Figure 4).

The Family 500+ program has been criticized for lowering female labor force participation and, by consequence, reinforcing gender roles. Initial analyses of its effects do point to a reduction of nearly 3 percentage points among women, with pronounced effects on low-educated mothers and those in small towns (Magda, Kiełczewska, and Brandt, 2018). While it is true that the reduction in labor market participation could have consequences for women's empowerment, including future participation and career progression, it is also true that such a policy relieves women of the double burden of paid and unpaid work and therefore reduces their time poverty.

Figure 5: Child Poverty Ratio, 2005–2019

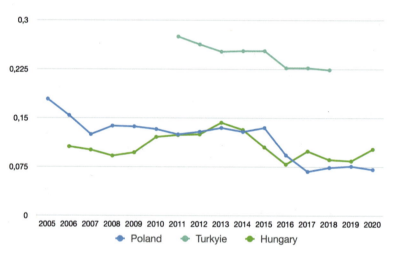

Source: OECD

Türkiye's pension and health reforms and cash-for-care

The principal social policies in Türkiye include pensions and social assistance. With respect to pensions, the government in 2003 doubled the value of social pensions for the elderly and disabled. In 2008, despite opposition from trade unions and other groups, the government reformed the social security system, merging employees, the self-employed, and civil servants into one social security system. The new system provided greater access and reduced inequality between groups to the benefit of the lower social classes, though later reforms tightened eligibility and removed the benefit floor (Szikra and Öktem, 2023). Another major flagship program that was highly appreciated by lower-income segments of the population was the reform of the health system, which effectively universalized access to public hospitals.

In addition, in 2006 the government enacted a cash-for-care program that provided cash transfers to a family member, usually a woman, in exchange for care at home of the elderly and the disabled (Buğra, 2020). The policy, which critics argue reinforces family-based care and the patriarchy (Akkan, 2018), grew from 28,583 beneficiaries in 2007 to 535,805 in 2021. Moreover, the administration of social assistance was often discretionary and administered by religious associations and thus "mired in clientelism" (Szikra and Öktem, 2023, p. 10).

While the cash-for-care program was not linked to a pro-natalist effort, the AKP has been openly committed to increasing birth rates, supported through financial compensation but also through de facto restrictions on family planning and abortion.[12] In addition, since 2015 the government has offered monetary incentives to raise the natality rate under the "Family and Dynamic Population Structure Conservation Program". These incentives, which are less generous than those provided in Hungary and Poland, provide a modest one-time payment at birth (Dildar, 2022).

While a more detailed analysis is needed to evaluate the impact of such policies on fertility, the de facto restrictions on family planning and abortion in Türkiye seem to have had a greater effect on raising fertility than the one-time monetary incentive. As Figure 4 shows, the fertility rate in Türkiye slightly increases after 2012 and starts to decline in 2015, the year in which the monetary incentives were initiated. In Poland, the fertility rate increased only slightly after the implementation of the Family 500+

---

12   In speeches, Erdoğan has condemned family planning "as a conspiracy to eliminate the nation" and has advocated for families to have a minimum of three children. Though abortion has not been outlawed, it has become unavailable in many public hospitals and many public family planning centers are defunct (Kiliç, 2017).

program in 2016, only to later fade out. This increase likely reflects a shift in the time preference of families who were already planning to have children, rather than an incentive to have children (Cook et al., 2022). Moreover, the restrictive abortion law, which led to the death of a woman in Poland from sepsis in September 2021, has likely discouraged some women from getting pregnant. In Hungary, the effect of the financial incentive on fertility seems to be stronger, but more detailed analyses are needed to evaluate its efficacy.

What is evident, however, is the effect of the policies on child poverty, which in all three countries, but particularly in Poland, fell substantially (see Figure 5). Such dramatic effects not only translate into immediate improvements in the material well-being of families with children, but also result in medium- to long-term benefits for these children in terms of health as well as education, as it deters school leaving.

Conclusion: An illiberal turn that has delivered

It is difficult to attribute success to governments that are explicitly pursuing anti-democratic agendas that will likely be experienced for decades to come. Nonetheless, it is important to understand how specific policies enacted by anti-democratic governments garner popular support. Specifically, it is important to ask the question of whether the illiberal turn experienced in these countries has nonetheless successfully responded to the economic needs of the middle and lower classes who constitute the base of the regimes' support, apart from the nationalist and conservative rhetoric, which has strong appeal to substantial parts of the population.

During their time in office, the Fidesz government of Hungary, PiS in Poland, and the AKP in Türkiye have continued with the neoliberal economic policies that they inherited, while at the same time pursuing economic, labor, and social policies that achieve the economic and social objectives laid out in their economic vision. Through political allies, the governments have been able to exercise direct or indirect control of key industries, including banking, energy, telecommunications, and the media. Hungary and Türkiye have both increased labor market flexibility, while Poland has only made piecemeal attempts to address its high degree of labor market segmentation. Unionization is weak in all three countries, and trade unionists have been attacked in Turkey. Nevertheless, the three governments have eagerly pursued increases in the minimum wage that have surpassed the rate of productivity growth. Meanwhile the economic insecurity resulting from the neoliberal economic and labor market policies are softened by large scale, highly visible, and highly popular social policies. Social spending strengthens support for the different regimes and reinforces their nationalist objectives of increased fertility and traditional gender roles. Absent large-scale economic crises, or if economic crises can be controlled – as Türkiye tenuously seems to be doing – it is hard to imagine such support withering.

References

Akkan, Başak. 2021. "Global Pandemic and the Veiled Crisis of Care in Turkey: Politics of Social Reproduction and Masculinist Restoration". *Historical Social Research / Historische Sozialforschung* 46(4): 31–49. https://www.jstor.org/stable/27081873.

Arsel, Murat, Fikret Adaman, and Alfredo Saad-Filho. 2021. "Authoritarian Developmentalism: The Latest Stage of Neoliberalism?". *Geoforum* 124 (August): 261–66. https://doi.org/10.1016/j.geoforum.2021.05.003

Artner, Annamaria. 2016. "Inside Hungary's Work-Based Society". *Social Europe (blog)*: https://www.socialeurope.eu/inside-hungarys-work-based-society.

Berberoglu, Berch. 2021. *The Global Rise of Authoritarianism in the 21st Century: Crisis of Neoliberal Globalization and the Nationalist Response*. New York: Routledge.

Buğra, Ayşe. 2020, "Politics of Social Policy in a Late Industrializing Country: The Case of Turkey". *Development and Change* 51(2): 442–462. https://doi.org/10.1111/dech.12566

Çelik, Aziz. 2015. "Turkey's New Labour Regime under the Justice and Development Party in the First Decade of the Twenty-First Century: Authoritarian Flexibilization". *Middle Eastern Studies* 51(4): 618–635.

Çelik, Aziz. 2019. "Sembiyotik İlişkiler ve Otoriter Korporatizm Kıskacında 2010'lu Yıllarda Türkiye'de Sendikalaşma, Toplu Pazarlık ve Grev Eğilimleri". *International Journal of Management Economics and Business* 15(15), 39–69. https://doi.org/10.17130/ijmeb.2019CEEIK201854097

Cook, Linda J., Elena R. Iarskaia-Smirnova, and Vladimir A. Kozlov. 2023. "Trying to Reverse Demographic Decline: Pro-Natalist and Family Policies in Russia, Poland and Hungary". *Social Policy and Society* 22(2): 355–75. https://doi.org/10.1017/S1474746422000628

Curtis, Karen. 2021. "100 Years of the ILO in Action: Reflections on Inclusive Collective Representation and the Organization's Quest for Social Justice". *King's Law Journal* 32(2): 183–96. https://doi.org/10.1080/09615768.2021.1969756

Dildar, Yasemin. 2022. "The Effect of Pronatalist Rhetoric on Women's Fertility Preferences in Turkey". *Population and Development Review* 48(2): 579–612. https://doi.org/10.1111/padr.12466

Fabry, Adam. 2019. *The Political Economy of Hungary: From State Capitalism to Authoritarian Neoliberalism*, London: Palgrave. https://doi.org/10.1007/978-3-030-10594-5

Fabry, Adam. 2021. "Neoliberalism, Crisis, and Authoritarian-Ethnicist Politics. The Consolidation of the Orbán Regime in Hungary", in Berch Berberoglu (ed.), *The Global Rise of Authoritarianism in the 21st Century: Crisis of Neoliberal Globalization and the Nationalist Response*. New York: Routledge.

Fischer, Andrew M. 2020. "The Dark Sides of Social Policy: From Neoliberalism to Resurgent Right-Wing Populism". *Development and Change* 51(2): 371–97. https://doi.org/10.1111/dech.12577.

Funke, Manuel, Schularick, Moritz, and Trebesch, Christoph. 2020. "Populist Leaders and the Economy". CEPR Discussion Paper No. DP15405, Available at SSRN: https://ssrn.com/abstract=3723597

Geva, Dorit. 2021. "Orbán's Ordonationalism as Post-Neoliberal Hegemony". *Theory, Culture & Society* 38(6): 71–93. https://doi.org/10.1177/0263276421999435.

Grzymala-Busse, Anna. 2017. "Global Populisms and Their Impact". *Slavic Review* 76(S1): S3–8. https://www.jstor.org/stable/26564940

Guriev, Sergei, and Elias Papaioannou. 2022. "The Political Economy of Populism". *Journal of Economic Literature* 60(3): 753–832. https://doi.org/10.1257/jel.20201595

Henley, Jon. 2021. "Hungary's Fidesz Party to Leave European Parliament Centre-Right Group". *The Guardian*, 3 March 2021. https://www.theguardian.com/world/2021/mar/03/hungarys-fidesz-party-to-leave-european-parliament-centre-right-group

Hungler, Sara. 2022. "Labor Law Reforms after the Populist Turn in Hungary". *Review of Central and East European Law* 47(1): 84–114. https://doi.org/10.1163/15730352-bja10063

ILO, 2020. Global Wage Report 2020–21: *Wages and minimum wages in the time of COVID-19*, International Labour Office – Geneva.

IMF, 2017. "The public works schemes in Hungary: Achievement and policy challenges", IMF e-library.

International Press Institute. 2023. "Analysis: One Year after Election, Media Freedom in Hungary Remains Suffocated". *International Press Institute* (blog). https://ipi.media/analysis-one-year-after-election-media-freedom-in-hungary-remains-suffocated/

ITUC, 2023. *Global Rights' Index*, Brussels.

Kılıç, Azer. 2017. "Abortion Politics and New Pro-Natalism in Turkey". *The Progressive Post* (blog). https://progressivepost.eu/abortion-politics-new-pro-natalism-turkey/

Kirişci, Kemal and Amanda Sloat. 2019. "The Rise and Fall of Liberal Democracy in Turkey: Implications for the West", *Brookings Policy Brief*.

Lendvai-Bainton, Noemi and Dorota Szelewa. 2021. "Governing New Authoritarianism: Populism, Nationalism and Radical Welfare Reforms in Hungary and Poland". *Social Policy & Administration* 55(4): 559–72. https://doi.org/10.1111/spol.12642

Ministry of Labour (Türkiye). 2014. "National Employment Strategy", 2014–2023.

Myck, Michał and Kajetan Trzciński. 2019. "From Partial to Full Universality: The Family 500+ Programme in Poland and its Labor Supply Implications", *DICE Report*, 17(3): 36–44.

Özkiziltan, Didem. 2019. "Authoritarian neoliberalism in AKP's Turkey: an industrial relations perspective". *Industrial Relations Journal* 50(3): 218–39. https://doi.org/10.1111/irj.12248

Orenstein, Mitchell and Bojan Bugaric. 2020. "Work, Family, Fatherland:The Political Economy of Populism in Central and Eastern Europe", LEQS Paper 163.

Riedel, Rafał. 2019. "Populism Is the Only Game in Town: Poland's Illiberal Turn as an Authoritarian Threat". *Sicherheit Und Frieden (S+F) / Security and Peace* 37(1): 24–28. https://www.jstor.org/stable/26679774

Sebők, Miklós and Jasper Simons. 2022. "How Orbán Won? Neoliberal Disenchantment and the Grand Strategy of Financial Nationalism to Reconstruct Capitalism and Regain Autonomy". *Socio-Economic Review* 20(4): 1625–51. https://doi.org/10.1093/ser/mwab052

Smiecinska, Nadia. 2021. "Crisis of Neoliberalism and the Rise of Authoritarianism in Poland: How a 'Good Change' is Turning Poland into a Neo-Authoritarian State", in Berch Berberoglu (ed.), *The Global Rise of Authoritarianism in the 21st Century: Crisis of Neoliberal Globalization and the Nationalist Response*. New York: Routledge.

Szanyi, Miklos. 2020. "Seeking the Best Master: State Ownership in the Varieties of Capitalism". Budapest: Central European University Press. https://muse.jhu.edu/pub/234/oa_edited_volume/book/76670

Szikra, Dorottya and Kerem Gabriel Öktem. 2023. "An Illiberal Welfare State Emerging? Welfare Efforts and Trajectories under Democratic Backsliding in Hungary and Turkey". *Journal of European Social Policy* 33(2): 201–15. https://doi.org/10.1177/09589287221141365

Vidra, Zsuzsanna. 2018. "Hungary's Punitive Turn: The Shift from Welfare to Workfare". *Communist and Post-Communist Studies* 51(1): 73–80. https://www.jstor.org/stable/48610502

Waddington, Jeremy, Torsten Müller, and Kurt Vandaele (eds.). 2023. *Trade Unions in the European Union*. Brussels: Peter Lang Verlag. https://doi.org/10.3726/b20254

Corporate Majoritarianism in India

SHEBA TEJANI
King's College London

I. Introduction

The Hindu nationalist Bharatiya Janata Party (BJP) came to power in India in 2014, riding on the wave of Modi's credentials as a *vikas purush*, or development man, of the state of Gujarat. As the architect of the "Gujarat model of development", Modi became known for executing infrastructure and urban renewal projects, promoting big business, and increasing economic growth. His Gujarat administration was known as being market-friendly and business-friendly, but contrary to expectations Modi did not implement major neoliberal economic reforms during his first term as prime minister. After his government was branded by the opposition as running a *suit-boot ki sarkar*, or a government that catered to the interests of the rich, and the BJP lost two state elections in 2015, Modi began to position himself as a "pro-poor" leader (Aiyar, 2019). Despite the BJP's criticism of the previous United Progressive Alliance (UPA) government's welfare "handouts", Modi embraced a range of welfare policies to boost his political support among the poor, which also proved to be electorally advantageous (Deshpande et al., 2019). Some of these were new initiatives while others were UPA schemes that were rebranded and relaunched as the prime minister's gift to the poor, such as the PM-Jan Dhan Yojana, PM-Ujjala Yojana, Ayushman Bharat, Awas Yojana, and the Swachch Bharat Abhiyan.[1]

This paper argues that Modi's ostensible pro-poor pivot has occurred alongside other concurrent shifts that are critical to understanding the character of the current political-economic regime. These are: i) the degradation and deregulation of labour rights through a new Labour Code; ii) the deepening of an oligarchic economic structure that has a symbiotic relationship with the BJP; and iii) intensifying anti-minorityism in the form of targeted violence and exclusion that is now being institutionalized. These processes are establishing a "corporate majoritarian" regime in India: a Hindu majoritarian state that is funded by big business, hostile to labour rights, and violent towards minorities.

II. Economic vision

With its competing objectives and imperatives, the BJP's economic policy agenda in its first term (2014–2019) has been characterised as "inconsistent and rambling" (Echeverri-Gent et al., 2019, p. 404). In its second term (2019–present), the government introduced a Covid stimulus package in May 2020 and branded it as part of the *Atmanirbhar Bharat Abhiyan* – a new drive to make India self-reliant. Self-reliance harks back to an older discourse of economic development that typically involved a large public sector and the use of trade and industrial policy to promote domestic enterprise. While the government claims that its notion of self-reliance is not a return to "old school protectionism" (Economic Survey, 2022, p. 34), it has kept the outlines of the vision vague and lumped together a mishmash of policies under this umbrella (Economic Survey, 2021, pp. 35–37). Apart from the inclusion of industrial policy packages for 10 sectors, many of these self-reliance policies could more accurately be described as conventionally neoliberal, featuring such aspects as liberalization of the agricultural sector, deregulation of labour, privatization of public sector undertakings (PSUs) in non-strategic sectors,

---

[1] These schemes include access to banking facilities, free cooking gas, subsidised credit for affordable housing, and construction of toilets to eliminate open defecation.

reduction of subsidies, use of public–private partnerships (PPP) in infrastructure, and enhancing the ease of doing business by creating a fast-track investment process.

In the 2022–2023 Economic Survey (2023) released by the Indian Ministry of Finance, the government once again announced the principles underlying its reforms over the last eight years but seemed to abandon the self-reliance framing. Rather it claimed its economic principles were *sabka saath, sabka vikas* or inclusive progress: a "paradigm shift in the growth and development strategy of the government, with the emphasis towards building partnerships amongst various stakeholders" (p. 28). This vision now centres the "ease of doing business" and "ease of living" as priorities of the government as illustrated by the Economic Survey 2022–2023. It aims to create this ease through the promotion of private sector participation, provision of public sector goods (particularly infrastructure), "trust-based governance", and by raising agricultural productivity (Figure 1, Economic Survey, 2023, p. 28). According to the survey, digitalization and flexibility will allow the ease of business and living to translate into greater efficiency and productivity.

Core components of the government's economic vision then are undergirding and fuelling the rise of corporate majoritarianism in India: the focus on large PPP projects is deepening the power of big business and the emphasis on flexibility and trust-based governance is undermining labour rights. The language of "ease" is a gesture towards the new middle classes, who value a smooth lifestyle, as well as to business interests, which had complained of obstructionism during the previous UPA regime. It is telling that the government identifies poverty as a problem yet argues that economic growth in India is inequality-reducing in nature and does not need to be explicitly tackled through policy (Economic Survey, 2021, pp. 122–143). Below I discuss the three key shifts that are establishing a corporate majoritarian regime in India.

III. Degradation of labour rights through the Labour Code

In 2019 and 2020, the government pushed through sweeping changes to India's labour regime by replacing 29 existing labour laws with 4 new laws known collectively as the Labour Code. The new laws are the Code on Wages, 2019; the Occupational Safety, Health and Working Conditions Code, 2020; the Industrial Relations Code, 2020; and the Code on Social Security, 2020. The idea of overhauling India's labour regime was first mooted in 2002 by the National Commission on Labour under a BJP-led coalition to improve "ease of compliance and ensure uniformity in labour laws" (PRS, 2023). There was some rationale for simplification as the laws lacked universal coverage and were sometimes inconsistent or even contradictory as labour is a concurrent subject on which both states and the central government can legislate. The result was often a thicket of laws that were poorly implemented and monitored. Labour flexibility has also become an important component of the government's strategy to attract investment from leading firms in global value chains that are diversifying out of China.

While the Code on Wages was passed in 2019, the remaining three laws were pushed through in September 2020 with little to no debate at a time when the opposition was boycotting parliament on another set of controversial farm laws (Rajalakshmi, 2020). Central unions had successfully blocked the passage of the Industrial Relations Code (IRC) through a nation-wide strike in 2015, but there has been little consultation with unions on the laws in general (Bhowmik, 2015). All central unions, including the BJP-affiliated Bharatiya Mazdoor Sangh, have opposed the codes while business associations have welcomed them (Alam, 2020). Most states have published draft rules based on the laws, but the Labour Ministry is holding belated talks with central unions to avoid disruption when the code is finally implemented (Haq, 2023). This now seems likely to occur only after the national elections in 2024.

I argue that the new Labour Code degrades workers' rights in the guise of simplification, uniformity, and flexibility. The Code skews bargaining power further towards capital, and away from labour in a context where the labour market is already in distress, informality and precarity is high, and labour standards are observed mostly in the breach. The laws significantly weaken associational rights, dilute and downgrade minimum wage protections, and facilitate increasing precarity. There are arbitrary exclusions and regimes of exceptions that make it difficult for workers to claim rights and monitor violations. The regulatory role of the state and its responsibility for oversight has been further reduced. Below I discuss some of the major limitations of different components of the Labour Code.

The IRC allows for the formal recognition and registration of unions, which is a welcome development, but it does so without defining a timeframe for registration and, using vague language, allows authorities to cancel union registrations (Bhuta, 2022). These weaknesses can be used to delay the recognition of unions or to deregister recalcitrant unions. The IRC restricts the right to strike by requiring a notice period of 60 days, which previously only applied to public utilities, and forbids strikes once adjudication starts – and even for a period after the process ends. The government can exempt any establishment from the IRC in case of emergency or in the public interest, which hands significant discretionary power to the government, enabling it to tamper with workers' rights (Sood, 2020).

The Wage Code, 2019, gives the central government a free hand to set the floor wage without committing to specific norms or principles (Clause 9). The law ignores the needs-based formula set out by the Indian Labour Conference as a guide to set minimum wages (Jayaram, 2019). It does not bode well in this regard that the Labour Ministry increased the minimum wage to INR 178 (USD 2.16) in 2019 – a paltry increase of INR 2 over two years – despite the Labour Conference's recommendation of INR 375 (USD 4.55) (Jayaram, 2019). Governments are required to constitute Advisory Boards consisting of employers, employees, and independent members to advise them on the setting of wages, but their advice is non-binding and only one-third of the members must be women (Clause 42). The Code expands the working day through the backdoor by creating exceptions to normal working hours that do not apply in emergencies, and for preparatory or complementary work (Wage Code, 2019, Clause 13). Although it increases the compensation for overtime, extending the working day in this way makes overtime pay harder to claim. The law also allows for the deduction of wages in the form of fines and to cover damages or amenities, which can encourage misuse and permit wage theft (Clause 18).

The Occupational Safety, Health and Working Conditions Code (OSH) creates a new category of "fixed term employment" (FTE) that permits the use of contract labour in core activities by creating exceptions to the law, when such labour was previously allowed in non-core activities only (Clause 57). FTE workers can be fired without notice, are not entitled to retrenchment compensation, and cannot participate in strikes.

Under the previous Industrial Disputes Act, 1947, firms with more than 100 workers were required to prepare Standing Orders or certified rules of conduct that were binding for employers and workers on matters concerning wages, working conditions, retrenchment, etc. The IRC 2020 raised this limit to 300 workers with a section of workers now losing these protections. Similarly, the Social Security (SS) and OSH Codes only apply to specific categories of establishments.[2] They exclude some sectors, such as hotels and restaurants entirely, while the SS Code does not apply to mines at all, with no justification for this exclusion. Access to social security also remains fragmentary, with obligatory provident fund, pension, and medical insurance benefits available only to employees earning above an income threshold to be determined by the government (Sood, 2020). The government has also empowered itself to exempt any establishment from the IRC (Clause 39) and OSH Codes (Clause 58), as well as from several chapters of the SS Code.

Even though the previous labour regime was already partly hollowed out through state level exceptions and ineffective monitoring of labour laws (Agarwala, 2019), the new codes go a step further in institutionalizing labour's weaker position and enhancing the discretionary powers of the state.

IV. Consolidation of an oligarchy

A pro-business shift is discernible in Indian economic policy since the late 1970s, which intensified through the period of liberalization in the 1980s and 1990s (Kohli, 2012). More recently, Jaffrelot et al. (2019) have

---

2 The SS Code (2020, p. 7) only applies to establishments that employ more than 10 workers, if they use electric power, and to those that employ 20 workers if they don't use electric power. The OSH Code (2020, p. 6) applies to establishments that employ more than 20 workers if they use electric power and to those that employ 40 workers if they don't use electric power.

argued that Indian business groups wield agenda-setting power to shape the country's political and social future, in addition to the veto power they use to block changes threatening their interests. At the same time, an unprecedented level of economic concentration is emerging in India as the structure of capitalism becomes increasingly oligarchic. Damodaran (2020) has characterised this as a shift from entrepreneurial capitalism to "conglomerate capitalism", highlighting that while the former also involved clientelism of a regional nature, it was a dynamic, diverse, and churning landscape in contrast to the narrow and centralized concentration we see today. Acharya (2023) finds that the share of the top five conglomerates in total non-financial assets in India rose from 10% to 18% between 1991 and 2021, and that their industrial footprint expanded from 25 non-financial sectors to span 40 sectors. Two companies in particular stand out here: Reliance Industries Limited and the Adani Group, which are among the largest conglomerates in the country by revenue. Both firms have massive operations in Gujarat, which is where the Adani Group is headquartered, while Reliance is based in Mumbai. Reliance Industries is an established multinational conglomerate that grew rapidly in the 1980s and spans petrochemicals, energy, natural gas, retail, telecommunications, and media. During the BJP's rule from 2014 to 2023, the net wealth of Reliance's chairman, Mukesh Ambani, rose by 455% from USD 18.6 billion to USD 83.4 billion and he is now India's richest man – as well as the world's ninth richest billionaire (Forbes, 2024a).

The Adani Group has become one of India's largest infrastructure companies, with interests in coal mining, thermal power plants, ports, and green energy. It expanded at a meteoric rate fuelled by debt between 2000–2013, roughly during Modi's tenure as chief minister of Gujarat, as its turnover rose by 1324% from $400 million to $5.7 billion (Rajashekhar, 2013). The net worth of its founder and chairman Gautam Adani rose from USD 2.8 billion in 2014 to USD 90 billion in 2022, but subsequently dropped to USD 47.2 billion in 2023 due to an exposé detailed later in this section (Forbes, 2024b). Adani is a firm supporter of Modi and stood by him after the anti-Muslim pogrom that took place in Gujarat in 2002 when Modi was chief minister of the state. When the Confederation of Indian Industry (CII) criticized Modi's handling of the episode, Adani formed the breakaway "Resurgent Group of Gujarat" along with a handful of other industrialists to counter the CII and to assert their support for Modi (Rajshekhar, 2013). Since then, Modi has been relying increasingly on big business rather than the BJP's party structures for campaign funds (Rajashekhar, 2013). He has also promoted relative newcomer Adani as a counterweight to Mukesh Ambani, the chairman of Reliance Industries.

Below I describe the four main ways in which ostensibly independent state institutions took, or failed to take, steps resulting in outcomes that cemented the dominance of these two groups.

1. Awarded contracts and assets through irregular practices

In 2019, when the Airports Authority of India (AAI) floated tenders to lease six lucrative airports in the country to private players, the Adani Group won bids to operate all six although it had no prior experience in the sector. This award also went against recommendations from the Department of Economic Affairs and Indian government agency Niti Aayog that no single player should be awarded more than two airport contracts. The bidding process was reported as being irregular because it sidelined the role of the regulator, reduced obligations for bidders, and tweaked eligibility criteria (Nair, 2019; Scroll, 2021). In another instance, the University Grants Commission, a statutory body and regulator of higher education under the Ministry of Education, floated a scheme to award selected universities the status of "Institutes of Eminence" (IoE), which would grant them greater autonomy and confer significant advantages in India's increasingly competitive and lucrative higher education market. Reliance's Jio Institute was awarded the status before it came into existence through the creation of a greenfield investment route, and despite the criteria requiring that IoEs must enter the global top 500 university rankings in just 10 years (Roychowdhury, 2018). It beat many existing universities in achieving this status (HT, 2018).

2. Made regulatory and policy changes that expanded the companies' market shares

A case in point is the launch of Reliance's telecom company Jio in 2018. The Telecom Regulatory Authority of India (TRAI), under the guise of testing network connectivity, allowed Jio to offer highly discounted pricing for 253 days without the risk of prosecution for predatory pricing (Stacey and Mundy, 2018). TRAI also made a steep 50% cut in the interconnection charge, which benefitted newcomer Jio as it had a relatively small subscriber base at the time (Srujana, 2019). As Jio rapidly gained market share, the regulator changed its definition of what constituted market power, which prevented the company from being subjected to predatory pricing rules and helped it to avoid tighter regulation and enhanced scrutiny. Jio now commands 37% of market share, which it has achieved in a record period of time (Grover, 2023).

3. Extended loans and equity through state-owned enterprises
The State Bank of India (SBI) approved a previously stalled USD 1 billion loan "under pressure" to the Adani Group in 2014 when half a dozen banks had declined to do so (NDTV, 2021). The bank currently has an exposure of USD 2.6 billion to the Adani Group (Das and Singh, 2023). In 2015, the Adani Group was described as "highly indebted" by Credit Suisse with a debt-equity ratio of 3.1 (Credit Suisse, 2015). Since then, state-owned enterprises have been infusing capital into various Adani projects by acquiring large equity stakes in them, often with no controlling interest (Mohammad, 2017). For instance, in 2017, the Indian Oil Corporation and the Gas Authority of India Limited (GAIL) invested 49% in a natural gas terminal valued at INR 60 billion in the state of Odisha, in which Adani Enterprises Ltd. has the controlling stake. Both firms had to borrow heavily for this (Nileena, 2018). Indian Oil also acquired a 50% stake in an INR 50.4 billion natural gas terminal at Mundra that is a joint venture between Adani Enterprises Ltd. and Gujarat State Petroleum Corporation (Nileena, 2018). In another instance, the State Bank of India (SBI) bought a 30% stake in Reliance's new banking venture Jio Payments Bank in 2018, through which Jio is to provide payment services on the SBI's digital banking application and gains access to its massive customer base (Rao, 2020).

4. Failed to pursue and prosecute irregularities
Investigations conducted since 2010 by the Directorate of Revenue Intelligence (DRI), Ministry of Finance, found that the Adani Group (among others) was over-invoicing imports of coal and power equipment to allegedly siphon profits to offshore accounts (Guha Thakurta, 2016;

The Wire, 2017; Nileena, 2018). According to Indian customs investigators' estimates, reported in the *Guardian*, Adani firms transferred INR 15 billion abroad just through power equipment imports, while costlier coal imports resulted in higher power tariffs for consumers (Safi, 2017; *The Wire*, 2017a; Guha Thakurta, 2016). However, in 2017 the DRI dropped all charges against the Adani Group, and although the Customs department challenged its order, the Supreme Court recently dismissed the case (*The Wire*, 2017b; *The Wire*, 2018; ET, 2024). The Securities and Exchange Board of India (SEBI) is currently investigating the Adani Group, on the direction of the Supreme Court, after the financial research firm Hindenburg Research alleged that the group was engaged in massive accounting fraud and stock manipulation (Upadhyay and Thomas, 2023; Joshi and Jain, 2023). SEBI's initial investigations "drew a blank" and petitioners in the case have alleged that it ignored earlier warnings and evidence from the DRI about Adani companies using offshore funds to manipulate stock markets (Tripathi, 2023).

There are numerous economic and political risks associated with the emergence of an oligarchy in India. Rising concentration curbs entrepreneurship and competitiveness in the economy as a handful of firms use state patronage to extract rents. In the Indian case, it also means that vital and strategic infrastructure is controlled by a few firms. The systemic financial and credit risks posed by large firms such as the Adani Group were amply demonstrated when the stock crash triggered by the publication of the Hindenburg report temporarily wiped out USD 86 billion from its stock value (Upadhyay and Thomas, 2023; Joshi and Jain, 2023). The group's debt is equivalent to approximately 1% of India's GDP with significant exposure of public institutions (Hanada, 2023).

Perhaps most critically for the future of democracy in the country, large private and anonymous political donations have allowed BJP's electoral juggernaut to thrive through an ingenious scheme introduced by the BJP in 2018 in the name of reforming electoral finance. Known as the electoral bond scheme, it allowed individuals and firms to buy interest-free bonds for donation to political parties anonymously and without limits (Biswas, 2022; Vaishnav, 2019). The names of donors were not part of the public record but because the public-sector SBI issued the bonds, it is likely that donor identities were available to the government. This scheme has also contributed to soaring election spending in India. The national elections of 2019, in which the BJP was elected for a second term, was the world's most expensive election yet with an estimated USD 8.6 billion spent in total (Gupta, 2019; Centre for Media Studies, 2019).

The Supreme Court did not hear legal petitions challenging the electoral bond scheme for six years in spite of its crucial implications for democracy. However, in February 2024 it struck down the scheme as unconstitutional and ordered the SBI to submit particulars of the transactions to the Election Commission of India (*Times of India*, 2024; *Mint*, 2024). During the writing of this paper, data released by the SBI showed that from 2019–2024, a total of INR 121.45 billion (USD 1.46 billion) was donated, of which roughly 50% or INR 60.61 (USD 727 million) went to the BJP, 12% to the Congress, and the rest to smaller parties (Kumar 2024; *The Wire*, 2024b). The data for 2018 has not been provided so these figures are incomplete. A company linked to Reliance Industries purchased electoral bonds worth INR 4 billion (USD 49.46 million), making it the fourth largest corporate donor, although its net profits were only a fraction of this amount (*The Wire*, 2024a; Reporter's Collective, 2024). Around 94% of this amount went to the BJP (*The Wire*, 2024b).

V. Intensifying anti-minorityism

The BJP is the political wing of the Hindu right-wing "family" of organizations known as the *Sangh Parivar*. *Hindutva*, or Hindu supremacy, is the main ideological plank of the Hindu right-wing, and it identifies religious minorities, especially Muslims, as enemies of the nation. The *Sangh Parivar* aims to turn India into a Hindu majoritarian state in which religious minorities have secondary status, and these aims are increasingly being realized with the BJP in power since 2014. I focus here on two ways in which religious minorities are losing their status as equal citizens: i) they are being targeted for intensified forms of exclusion and violence; ii) the exclusion of Muslims is being institutionalized through a new law called the Citizenship Amendment Act (2019), which uses religion as a criterion for citizenship and explicitly discriminates against Muslims.

Although popular support for Hindutva has been rising in India since the 1980s, the vilification and stigmatization of Muslims has reached new heights and acquired widespread legitimacy during this time. Malicious discourses about Muslims conducting holy war by taking over land and property ("land jihad"), ensnaring young Hindu girls into marriage to convert them to Islam ("love jihad"), and encroaching on Hindu business and trade ("*vyapar* jihad") are constantly circulating in the media and creating a cesspool of hatred (see, for instance, Mirchandani, 2018). In addition, a high-pitched nationalist discourse presents Muslims and Christians as inherently anti-national because of their religious affiliations, and associates them with the forced religious conversion of Hindus. Transnational discourses about "Islamic terror" are used as further evidence of Muslim aggression and capacity for violence.

As a result, religious minorities are facing an explosion of physical, social, and economic violence that is often state sponsored or supported, with perpetrators having almost complete impunity. The ban in many Indian states on the slaughter of cows and consumption of beef has unleashed targeted violence against Muslims and Dalits who are accused of violating these bans. Vigilante groups have lynched those suspected of illegally owning cattle, abducting cattle, and eating beef (Venkatesan, 2017). Police have either stalled investigations into these acts of violence or have been complicit in cover-ups due to political pressures. Most perpetrators are roaming free while survivors are thrown in jail for possessing or consuming meat (HRW, 2019; Hindutva Watch, 2023; Siasat Hate Tracker, 2023). There is a lack of systematic statistics on hate crimes based on religion other than independent media reports. Still, from 2014–2019, independent data gathering efforts revealed that 83 incidents of violence related only to cow vigilantism took place, in which 35 people were killed (mostly Muslim) and 127 people were injured (Hate Crime Watch, 2019). These are no doubt conservative estimates.

In BJP-ruled states and union territories, such as Uttar Pradesh (UP) and Kashmir, municipal governments have singled out Muslim property for demolition by alleging that they have encroached upon public land (Hassan and Ellis-Petersen, 2023; Bhushan, 2022). Such state-sponsored violence has earned the moniker "bulldozer politics" and the Chief

Minister of UP is popularly known as "bulldozer baba" for his brazen use of this method (Narayan, 2022). Muslims increasingly live in segregated communities in urban areas across India due to widespread housing discrimination or fear of violence (Gayer and Jaffrelot 2012; Tejani 2022). There have also been open calls for the socio-economic boycott of Muslims with a case recorded in Purola, Uttarakhand, where the alleged abduction of a Hindu girl by Muslim men was used as a pretext to call for the boycott of the whole Muslim community (Jafri, 2023). This has been accompanied by open calls for the extermination of Muslims, most recently at a meeting of religious leaders in Uttarakhand in 2022 (Jha, 2022).

In 2019, the government passed The Citizenship Amendment Act (CAA) with the stated aim of providing a pathway to citizenship for irregular migrants from Hindu, Sikh, Parsi, Jain, and Christian communities who had fled religious persecution in neighbouring Muslim majority countries, namely Pakistan, Afghanistan, and Bangladesh (BBC, 2024). The law explicitly excludes Muslims and undermines the secular character of India's constitution by using religion as a test for citizenship (Nagarwal, 2022). The BJP has been calling for a national citizenship verification process – the National Register of Citizens (NRC) – to be carried out across the country to identify irregular migrants (HRW, 2019). If it is implemented, Muslims who cannot provide the right documentation would effectively be disenfranchised and left stateless, while those belonging to other religions could apply for citizenship through the CAA. This NRC experiment has already been carried out in the state of Assam, where, at last count, 1.9 million people (including Hindus and Muslims) were excluded from the citizenship rolls (Chatterji et al., 2021). Although the implementation of the CAA was halted due to widespread protests across the country, the government announced rules to implement the law on 11 March 2024, on the same day the Supreme Court found that electoral bonds were unconstitutional. The move is being widely seen as an attempt to deflect attention from the electoral bonds issue and polarize the electorate before the national election (Sharma, 2024).

VI. Conclusion

The BJP government's economic policy approach is a mix of initiatives to boost big business and to deregulate and flexibilize sectors such as the labour market. Though it frames these policies in neoliberal economic terms, they are a combination of competition reducing and enhancing measures that concentrate economic and political power. This paper argues that the degradation of labour rights, consolidation of an oligarchy, and intensifying anti-minorityism are interrelated cornerstones of the emerging corporate majoritarian regime in India. The new Labour Code discipline workers through markets while allowing businesses to extract higher profits. For workers, political incorporation through *Hindutva* and benefits received through welfare policies can be a substitute for economic inclusion, for a time, though they will not solve the larger structural infirmities of the Indian economy. At the same time, economic concentration has facilitated political centralization and vice versa through the electoral bonds scheme, which has funnelled funds from big business to the BJP in an opaque way and without any democratic checks.

Support of the Hindu supremacist regime appears to pay handsomely for emerging oligarchs who are underwriting India's transformation into a Hindu majoritarian state. These oligarchs have continued supporting the BJP, even though it has ascended to power through consistent anti-Muslim mobilization, so long as the regime serves their interests and facilitates their growing economic power. Just as importantly, Hindu majoritarianism alters the nature of the state itself and makes it more malleable for capitalist accumulation through the unabashed use of coercive state power that can be exercised against any groups or individuals deemed to act against the "national interest", howsoever defined. These are mutually reinforcing tendencies though there are fragilities in this politico-economic formation, and new political mobilizations, a realigning of interests, or economic shifts could, potentially, destabilize its path.

References

Acharya, V. V. (2023). India at 75: Replete with contradictions, brimming with opportunities, saddled with challenges. *Brookings Papers on Economic Activity* (1): 185–288.

Agarwala, R. (2019). 'The Politics of India's Reformed Labor Model', in Christophe Jaffrelot, Atul Kohli, and Kanta Murali (eds), *Business and Politics in India*. Oxford University Press. https://doi.org/10.1093/oso/9780190912468.003.0004

Aiyar, Y. (2019). 'Modi Consolidates Power: Leveraging Welfare Politics'. *Journal of Democracy* 30(4): 78–88. https://doi.org/10.1353/jod.2019.0070

Alam, M. (2020). 'As Lok Sabha Approves Three Labour Codes, Workers' Unions Plan Protests', *The Wire*, 23 September 2020. https://thewire.in/government/lok-sabha-labour-codes-workers-union-protest

BBC (2024). 'CAA: India's new citizenship law explained'. https://www.bbc.co.uk/news/world-asia-india-50670393

Bhowmik, S. K. (2015). 'Protecting Employers against Workers and Trade Unions: New Bill on Industrial Relations'. *Economic and Political Weekly* 1(29): 15–18.

Bhushan, B. (2022). 'Political significance of Uttar Pradesh's bulldozer demolitions'. *Deccan Herald*, 16 June 2022. https://www.deccanherald.com/opinion/political-significance-of-uttar-pradesh-s-bulldozer-demolitions-1118558.html

Bhuta, A. (2022). 'Imbalancing Act: India's Industrial Relations Code, 2020'. *Indian Journal of Labour Economics* 65: 821–830.

Biswas, S. (2022). 'Electoral bonds: India's rocky road to transparency in political financing', *BBC News*, 3 October 2022. https://www.bbc.co.uk/news/world-asia-india-62991256

Block, D. (2019). 'Data plans: How government decisions are helping Reliance Jio monopolise the telecom sector', *The Caravan*, 1 February 2019. https://caravanmagazine.in/reportage/government-helping-reliance-jio-monopolise-telecom

Centre for Media Studies (2019). Poll expenditure, the 2019 elections. New Delhi: Centre for Media Studies.

Chatterji, A. P., Desai, M., Mander, H. and Azad, A. K. (2021). 'Detention, Criminalisation, Statelessness: The Aftermath of Assam's NRC', *The Wire*, 9 September 2021. https://thewire.in/rights/detention-criminalisation-statelessness-the-aftermath-of-assams-nrc

Damodaran, H. (2020). From 'entrepreneurial' to 'conglomerate' capitalism. Seminar, October 2020, 734: 33–37.

Das, S., Singh, P. (2023). 'Largest Indian Bank SBI Has $2.6 Billion of Loans to Adani', *Bloomberg*. https://www.bloomberg.com/news/articles/2023-02-02/largest-indian-bank-sbi-has-2-6-billion-of-loans-to-adani

Deshpande, R., Tillin, P., and Kailash, K. K. (2019). 'The BJP's Welfare Schemes: Did they make a difference in the 2019 elections?' *Studies in Indian Politics*, 7(2): 219–233.

Echeverri-Gent, J., Sinha, A., and Wyatt, A. (2021). 'Economic distress amidst political success: India's economic policy under Modi, 2014–2019'. *India Review* 20: 402–435.

Economic Survey (2021). *Economic Survey*, 2020–21, Ministry of Finance, Government of India, New Delhi.

Economic Survey (2022). *Economic Survey*, 2021–22, Ministry of Finance, Government of India, New Delhi.

Economic Survey (2023). *Economic Survey*, 2022–23. Ministry of Finance, Government of India, New Delhi.

ET (2024). 'SC junks review plea by customs on alleged overvaluation in import of capital goods by Adani firms', *The Economic Times*, 25 January 2024. https://economictimes.indiatimes.com/news/india/sc-junks-review-plea-by-customs-on-alleged-overvaluation-in-import-of-capital-goods-by-adani-firms/articleshow/107152555.cms?from=mdr

Forbes (2024a). Mukesh Ambani, Forbes Profile. https://www.forbes.com/profile/mukesh-ambani/

Forbes (2024b). Gautam Adani, Forbes Profile. https://www.forbes.com/profile/gautam-adani-1/

Gayer, L. and Jaffrelot, C. (eds). (2012). *Indians in Muslim cities: Trajectories of marginalization*. HarperCollins.

Ghosh, S., Marsh, A., and Sanjal P. R. (2021). SBI under pressure over loan to controversial Adani mine. *NDTV Profit*, 9 April 2021. https://www.ndtv.com/business/sbi-under-pressure-over-loan-to-controversial-adani-mine-2409649

Grover, J. (2023). 'Jio tops user additions in December, Airtel's gain highest in 9 months'. *Indian Express*, 17 February 2023. https://www.financialexpress.com/business/industry-jio-tops-user-additions-in-december-airtels-gain-highest-in-9-months-2984019/

Guha Thakurta, P. (2016). 'Power Tariff Scam Gets Bigger at Rs. 50,000 Crore as Allegations of Equipment Over-Invoicing Emerge', *The Wire*, 18 May 2016. https://thewire.in/business/power-tariff-scam-gets-bigger-at-rs-50000-crore

Gupta, A., Shah, K., and Kumar, P. (2015). 'House of Debt: Still in the Woods'. Asia-Pacific/ India, Equity Research, Credit Suisse, 21 October 2015.

Gupta, S. (2019). 'India's election spending surges past US to record high', CNN, 8 June 2019. https://edition.cnn.com/2019/06/08/asia/india-election-spending-intl/index.html

Hanada, R. (2023). 'Adani's debts exceed 1% of Indian economy'. *Nikkei Asia*. https://asia.nikkei.com/Business/Companies/Adani-Group/Adani-s-debts-exceed-1-of-Indian-economy

Hassan, A. and Ellis-Petersen, H. (2023). '"Bulldozer politics"': Modi's demolition drive fuels Muslims' fears in Kashmir'. *The Guardian*, 19 March 2023. https://www.theguardian.com/world/2023/mar/19/bulldozer-politics-modi-demolition-drive-fuels-muslims-fears-in-kashmir

Haq, Z. (2023). 'Implementation of 4 codes stalled'. *Hindustan Times*, 8 May 2023. https://www.hindustantimes.com/india-news/indias-sweeping-labour-code-implementation-stalled-until-2024-elections-101683485041321.html

Hindutva Watch (2023). Hindutva Watch. https://hindutvawatch.org

HRW (2019). Violent cow protection in India, Human Rights Watch. https://www.hrw.org/report/2019/02/19/violent-cow-protection-india/vigilante-groups-attack-minorities

HT (2018). 'Jio Institute, still on paper, gets "eminence" tag, sparks row', *Hindustan Times*, 10 July 2018. https://www.hindustantimes.com/india-news/still-on-paper-jio-institute-gets-institution-of-eminence-tag-draws-criticism/story-w45LROLHvX95uUB4eKdfXO.html

IE (2021). 'In 2019-20, BJP got 75% of poll bonds sold, Congress just 9%'. *Indian Express*, 10 August 2021. https://indianexpress.com/article/india/in-2019-20-bjp-got-75-per-cent-of-poll-bonds-sold-congress-just-9-per-cent-7446293/

Jafri, A. (2023). 'Cross marks on door, cries of extermination: How Uttarakhand became our hate speech capital.' *The Wire*, 12 June 2023. https://thewire.in/communalism/uttarakhand-hate-speech-jihad-anti-muslim

Jaffrelot, C., Kohli, A., and Murali, K. (2019). 'Conclusion', in Christophe Jaffrelot, Atul Kohli, and Kanta Murali (eds), *Business and Politics in India*. Oxford University Press.

Jaffrelot, C., Kohli, A., and Murali, K. (eds). *Business and Politics in India*. Oxford University Press.

Jayaram, N. (2019). 'Protection of Workers' Wages in India: An Analysis of the Labour Code on Wages, 2019'. *Economic and Political Weekly* 54.

Jha, D. K. (2022). Unholy Orders. *The Caravan*, 1 March 2022. https://caravanmagazine.in/commentary/haridwar-dharma-sansad-vhp-rss-hate-speech

Joshi, A. and Jain, A. (2023). 'Why are Adani shares falling?' *Forbes Advisor*, 14 June 2023. https://www.forbes.com/advisor/in/investing/why-adani-shares-are-falling/

Kohli, A. (2012). *Poverty amid plenty in the new India*. Cambridge University Press.

Kumar, A. (2024). 'Electoral bonds data: Here's how much the BJP, Congress and TMC received', *Business Standard*, 22 March 22024. https://www.business-standard.com/elections/lok-sabha-election/electoral-bonds-data-here-s-how-much-the-bjp-congress-and-tmc-received-124032200760_1.html

Mint (2024). 'SC strikes down electoral bonds scheme, directs bank to stop issuance of bonds: 5 key highlights', *Mint*, 15 February 2024. https://www.livemint.com/news/india/sc-judgment-on-electoral-bonds-scheme-dy-chandrachud-case-what-is-electoral-bonds-11707969926316.html

Mirchandani, M. (2018). 'Digital Hatred, Real Violence: Majoritarian Radicalisation and Social Media in India', ORF Occasional paper 167, Observer Research Foundation.

Mohammad, N. (2017). 'Does It Make Economic Sense for IOC and Gail India to Invest in Adani's LNG Terminals?' *The Wire*, 16 November 2017. https://thewire.in/business/indian-oil-gail-india-adani-lng-terminals

Nagarwal, N. (2022). The Citizenship Amendment Act 2019: An Insight through Constitutional and Secularism Perspective. *Journal of Asian and African Studies* 57(8): 1562–1576.

Nair, R. (2019). 'How Modi Bypassed Norms to Try and Enable Adani's Entry into Airport Business'. *Newsclick*, 27 March 2019. https://www.newsclick.in/Modi-Adani-Privatisation-of-Airports

Narayan, B. (2022). 'Why "Bulldozer baba" Yogi Adityanath keeps using the machine for law and order'. *The Print*, 17 June 2022. https://theprint.in/opinion/why-bulldozer-baba-yogi-adityanath-keeps-using-the-machine-for-law-and-order/1000182/

Nileena M. S. (2018). 'Coalgate 2.0', *The Caravan*, 1 March 2018. https://caravanmagazine.in/reportage/coalgate-2-0

PRS 2023 (n.d.). Overview of Labour Law Reforms. PRS Legislative Service. https://prsindia.org/billtrack/overview-of-labour-law-reforms

Rajalakshmi, T. K. (2020). 'The new labour codes: Labour's loss'. *Frontline*, 12 October 2020.

Rajshekhar, M. (2019). 'From 2014 to 2019: How the Adani Group's footprint expanded across India'. *Scroll*, 15 May 2019. https://scroll.in/article/923095/from-2014-to-2019-how-the-adani-groups-footprint-expanded-across-india

Rajshekhar, M. (2013). 'Gautam Adani: Meet the man who built Rs 47,000 crore infrastructure empire', *Economic Times*, 5 September 2013. https://economictimes.indiatimes.com/industry/indl-goods/svs/construction/gautam-adani-meet-the-man-who-built-rs-47000-crore-infrastructure-empire/articleshow/22304960.cms?from=mdr

Rao, V. V. (2020). 'The rise of monopolies in "New India"', *Deccan Herald*, 19 November 2020. https://www.deccanherald.com/opinion/the-rise-of-monopolies-in-new-india-917337.html

Reporter's Collective (2024). 'Confirmed: A Reliance Group company donated Rs 410 crores through electoral bonds', *Reporter's Collective*, 15 March 2024. https://www.reporters-collective.in/trc/company-with-reliance-links-third-largest-donor

Roy Chowdhury, S. (2018). 'Explainer: How Reliance's Jio Institute was chosen as an "Institution of Eminence"', *Scroll*, 12 July 2018. https://scroll.in/article/886166/explainer-how-reliances-jio-institute-was-chosen-as-an-institution-of-eminence

Safi, M. (2018). 'Adani Group files plea in India high court to stall fraud investigation', *The Guardian*, 29 August 2018. https://www.theguardian.com/business/2018/aug/29/adani-group-india-dri-investigation-plea

Scroll (2019). 'FactChecker pulls down hate crime database, IndiaSpend editor Samar Halarnkar resigns'. *Scroll*, 12 September 2019. https://scroll.in/latest/937076/factchecker-pulls-down-hate-crime-watch-database-sister-websites-editor-resigns

Scroll (2021). 'Adani Group won six airport bids despite finance ministry, NITI Aayog's objections: Indian Express'. *Scroll*. https://scroll.in/latest/984105/adani-group-won-six-airport-bids-despite-finance-ministry-niti-aayogs-objections-indian-express

Siasat (2023). 'Hate tracker 2022: A list of anti-Muslim incidents across India'. *The Siasat Daily*. https://www.siasat.com/hate-tracker-2022-a-list-of-anti-muslim-incidents-across-india-2489905/

Sharma, Y. (2024). '"Dark day": India on edge over religion-based citizenship law before polls', *Al Jazeera*, 12 March 2024. https://www.aljazeera.com/news/2024/3/12/dark-day-india-on-edge-over-religion-based-citizenship-law-before-polls

Sood, A. (2020). The Silent Takeover of Labour Rights. *The India Forum*, 17 November 2020. https://www.theindiaforum.in/article/silent-takeover-labour-rights

Srujana, B. (2019). 'The Billionaire Beneficiaries of BJP's Schemes', *Newsclick*, 3 May 2019. https://www.newsclick.in/BJP-Schemes-Modi-Ambani-Adani-Baba-Ramdev-Indian-Billionaire

Stacey, K. and Mundy, S. (2018). 'India: the creation of a mobile phone juggernaut'. *Financial Times*, 1 October 2018. https://www.ft.com/content/4297df22-bcfa-11e8-94b2-17176fbf93f5

Tejani, S. (2023). 'Saffron geographies of exclusion: The Disturbed Areas Act of Gujarat'. *Urban Studies* 60(4): 597–619.

The Wire (2017a). 'Adani Group Moved Rs 1,500 Crore to Offshore Haven, Alleges Customs Report'. *The Wire*, 16 August 2017. https://thewire.in/168530/adani-black-money-mauritius-siphon-rs-1500-crore/?relatedposts_hit=1&relatedposts_origin=198442&relatedposts_position=0

The Wire (2017b). 'Customs Agency's Case Against Adani Group Dealt Setback', *The Wire*, 25 August 2017. https://thewire.in/business/customs-agencys-case-adani-group-dealt-setback

The Wire (2018). 'Customs Department Challenges DRI Authority's Clean Chit to Adani Firms', *The Wire*, 12 February 2018. https://thewire.in/business/customs-department-challenges-dri-authoritys-clean-chit-adani-firms

The Wire (2024a). 'Lottery, Infra, Mining, Real Estate Firms Top Electoral Bonds Chart but No Info on Who Paid Whom', *The Wire*, 14 March 2024. https://thewire.in/government/election-commission-uploads-electoral-bonds-data

The Wire (2024b). 'Electoral Bonds: Ek Prem Katha', *The Wire*. https://thewire.in/electoral-bond

Tripathi, A. (2023). 'Sebi suppressed facts about Adani stock manipulation, Supreme Court told', *Deccan Herald*, 11 September 2023. https://www.deccanherald.com/india/sebi-suppressed-facts-and-slept-over-dri-information-on-stock-manipulation-by-adani-petitioner-tells-sc-2681801

Upadhyay, J. P. and Thomas, C. (2023). 'Indian regulator looking into $86 billion Adani share wipeout'. *Reuters*, 2 February 2023. https://www.reuters.com/business/adani-group-stocks-resume-fall-after-25-bln-share-sale-goes-through-2023-02-01/

Vaishnav, M. (2019). 'Electoral Bonds: The Safeguards of Indian Democracy Are Crumbling'. Carnegie Endowment for International Peace. https://carnegieendowment.org/2019/11/25/electoral-bonds-safeguards-of-indian-democracy-are-crumbling-pub-80428

Venkatesan, R. (2017). 'Laws Prohibiting Cow Slaughter are Creating Both Vigilantes and Victims', *The Wire*, 15 September 2017. https://thewire.in/politics/cow-slaughter-laws-vigilantes-victims

Conclusion:
Towards a Democratic Economics

The papers in this publication of THE NEW are based on the project "Beyond Neoliberalism and Neo-illiberalism: Economic Policies and Performance for Sustaining Democracy". They point to the need for a more sustained effort to counter both the economic insecurity and volatility of neoliberalism and the labor suppression, ethno-nationalism, and clientelism of the neo-illiberal economies. Such an effort will require creative and interdisciplinary work on both theory and policy.

The word democracy is ill-defined in economics and certainly not well understood in the economics profession. At the same time, it is widely acknowledged that economic forces, resulting in part from neoliberal policy, were partly responsible for the backlash against democracy over the last 15 years. This backlash is the illiberal turn that has occurred across the countries discussed in this book. Karl Polanyi's 1944 classic *The Great Transformation* provides a useful lens for understanding the illiberal turn in the 21st century. Polanyi showed that liberal free market capitalism inevitably creates a political backlash – what he referred to as a "pendulum swing" – but that the backlash could be to the right or the left, that is towards authoritarianism or towards social democracy. The liberal period from 1870–1913, followed by World War I and the Great Depression, led to fascism in the 1930s. Polanyi argued that it was the commodification of labor, money, and nature – what he called the three fictitious commodities – that underpinned this authoritarian turn. His account serves as a warning that failure to resist this commodification of important human needs and functions will lead to the authoritarian rather than the democratic response.

The future of this project will focus on the Polanyian question of how economic policy might be reformed to both sustain growth and provide more equality, while underpinning democratic politics and society. We have identified some of the common economic policies in the illiberal countries: protectionism and anti-immigrant policies, labor suppression, support of oligarchic elites and targeted social programs to support population growth and to provide electoral support. The latter often combines clientelism with ethno-nationalism.

There is a clear need for a positive political economy that would apply to both neoliberal and neo-illiberal governments, not just an economic policy regime that only works with one set of institutions. The next phase of this New School project will seek to build out the core of this positive political agenda by answering some basic questions, including:

1. How do we stabilize the crisis-prone capitalist economy? Several participants stressed the need for a progressive vision of full employment with good, stable jobs that also would aid productivity growth;
2. How can progressive democratic governments around the world find stable and equitable economic policies when the global economy is dominated by the US and outdated and overly liberal international economic institutions? Governments with progressive, equity-oriented goals are constrained by tax, trade, finance, and central bank policies. How can the international economic institutions, which have diminished in effectiveness and lost a sense of their mission, be reconstituted for the new era?, and;
3. What are the macroeconomics consistent with these first two points? How do we develop macro policies that support growth with explicit attention to equitable distribution of income and stability? Can we move beyond the "Keynesian straitjacket" and New Deal consensus into some new policy areas? The task is to show how this policy program can deliver economic growth which could then support conditions for democracy.

In our next phase, we intend to undertake deeper research on labor market policies on full employment and the creation of networks of policy makers, scholars, and advocates working at the national level to share ideas on national and international policy.

We are left with two even more basic questions: What are the economic conditions for political or social democracy? What are the political conditions for economic justice and sustainability? Connecting economics and economic policy to the future of democracy is a key goal in the pursuit of social justice. One thing we have learned so far in this project is that economists today are not well prepared to address the topic of democracy. In the future, it will be important for the study of economy and democracy to be brought even more closely together.

WILLIAM
MILBERG
The New School

List of Contributors

David Autor
Massachusetts Institute of Technology, United States of America

Janine Berg
International Labour Office, Switzerland

Laura Carvalho
Open Society Foundations, United States of America

Thiemo Fetzer
University of Warwick, United Kingdom and University of Bonn, Germany

Manuel Funke
Kiel Institute for the World Economy, Germany

Daniela Gabor
University of the West of England, Bristol, United Kingdom

Markus Gabriel
THE NEW INSTITUTE, Germany

Darrick Hamilton
The New School, United States of America

Anna Katsman
THE NEW INSTITUTE, Germany

Brian Kettenring
Hewlett Foundation, United States of America

Thomas Liess
The New School, United States of America

William Milberg
The New School, United States of America

Rosana Pinheiro-Machado
University College Dublin, Ireland

Jessica Pisano
The New School, United States of America

Dani Rodrik
Kennedy School, Harvard University, United States of America

Moritz Schularick
Kiel Institute for the World Economy, Germany and Sciences Po, France

Joseph Stiglitz
Columbia University, United States of America

Sheba Tejani
King's College London, United Kingdom

Christoph Trebesch
Kiel Institute for the World Economy, Germany

Ludovica Tursini
The New School, United States of America

Ayca Zayim
Mount Holyoke College, United States of America

With staff support from Richard McGahey, Abhik Sengupta, and Michael Tedesco from The New School

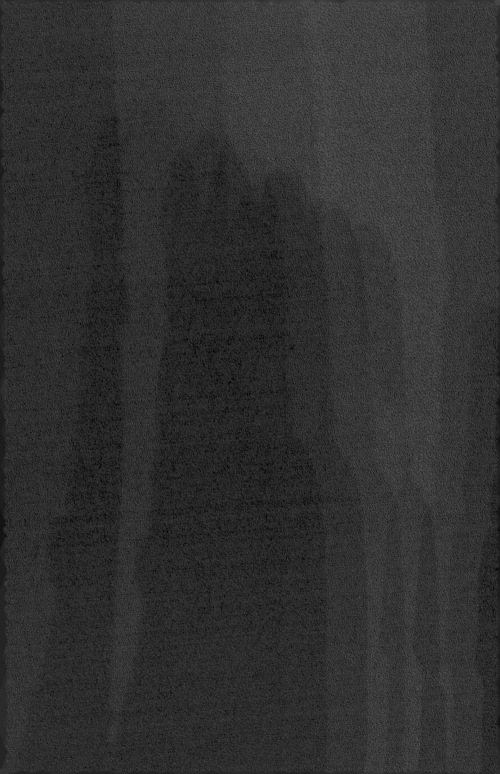